Faces of our Time

Faces of our Time

YOUSUF KARSH

University of Toronto Press / Toronto and Buffalo

PRINTED IN THE NETHERLANDS BY JOH. ENSCHEDÉ EN ZONEN, HAARLEM

ISBN 0-8020-1771-1

MICROFICHE ISBN 0-8020-0101-7

LC 79-155956

To my wife Estrellita
whose creativity and perceptive insight
have richly contributed to
every phase of my life

Contents

Introduction

It was André Malraux, I believe, who first described books as museums without walls. Books can carry, through reproduction, man's art and achievements, past and present, to a larger public than ever could see the originals in their gallery-homes. This power of the printed page explains the thrill I feel at the publication of a third volume of my portraits of the world's great men and women. The first volume in this informal series, *Portraits of Greatness*, issued in 1959, still towers as a landmark in my career. Photographs are an art form—I believe that statement at last is no longer arguable—that is as demanding of fidelity in reproduction as any Bach cantata or highly chromatic canvas. In these books, through care and refined technology, this aim is realized. As a result, tens of thousands of people around the world have been enabled to study the qualities I found in the subjects of my pictures, not in just broad outlines, but seeing the fine detail, the subtle gradations, the delicate nuances of light and shadow. My ambition as a portrait photographer has always been to bring people together, hopefully for a meeting of minds. I am happy if the understanding viewer feels that, through my photograph, he has intimately encountered a new dimension in a great personality, that in a more profound way he knows Hemingway, or Einstein, or Churchill, or Helen Keller.

By a strange twist, in the four years since the publication of the second volume, *Karsh Portfolio*, I have also been able to reach more people than ever before with actual prints from my darkroom—in museums *with* walls! This development began at EXPO '67, the world's fair held so brilliantly in Montreal in Canada's Centennial year. I was invited to prepare a one-man show (the only one by an artist at the fair) of over 100 photographs of world personalities, each photograph with my own descriptive caption. In the next year the exhibition was shown at the Montreal Museum of Fine Arts: the opening was on a cold, wintry, January night, yet so many people were anxious to get in that the line-up extended twice around the block. Then came an event that was particularly gratifying, for in April the exhibition opened at the Boston Museum of Fine Arts. It was in Boston that as a youth I studied for three years in the studio of that supreme photographic portraitist, John H. Garo, and it is in Boston's museums and galleries that I first encountered the cultural treasures of the world after a boyhood in the poverty of Armenia: this was a small thanksgiving. And again, so popular was the exhibition that several extra guards were engaged for the last week to handle traffic through the galleries. The exhibition has since travelled to the Corning Museum, the Detroit Institute of Fine Arts, and the Seattle Art Museum; as I write it has crossed the Atlantic and is touring European centres, and will soon tour Midwest America.

At every stage the exhibition has been augmented with new portraits of personalities who have assumed prominence or whom I have been able to meet and photograph. My search to portray greatness continues without abatement after more than three decades. Recently, it has extended to the East. I was invited to be photographic adviser to EXPO '70, the international exhibition at Osaka; and with this opportunity I set out to photograph some of Japan's 'living human treasures,' for so the people of that country designate their most revered artists and scientists. Those portraits were added to a second exhibition of my prints which toured the principal cities of Japan in 1970, and which has since been presented by the Canadian government at Japan's request to the Museum of Modern Art in Tokyo. Two of the portraits appear in this volume.

And so I now enjoy two parallel and mutually-reinforcing media for reaching a wider public through my work. In this volume, the reader will forgive me, I hope, if some faces are familiar. They are the faces of old friends of all of us. The qualities of greatness that make a Casals, a Sibelius, a Schweitzer are not so common that they can be eclipsed or ignored even within a full generation. Other photographs I have retained are classics, without which I can scarcely conceive any representation of my work. There are many new faces. Among them are the political leaders of the United States and Canada, Nixon and Trudeau. There are the Columbuses of our times: explorers of extraterrestrial space, the crew of Apollo XI; pioneers within the body of man, Barnard and DeBakey; the intellectual adventurer, McLuhan. However, the majority of the new faces, young and very old, photographed on three continents, are of artists: great figures of sculpture, painting, music, drama, and photography. For artists are the most intriguing and unpredictable of personalities. They are, for the most part, very private, often highly individualistic, dedicated to a lonely and intensely personal quest for excellence in their chosen medium. To capture these qualities when they are in abundance is both challenging and immensely satisfying.

The words I wrote in my introduction to *Karsh Portfolio* are still applicable, for the qualities of greatness do not change: 'The fascination of the men and women portrayed in this book lies beneath the surface of their features, no matter how striking these may be; it lies beyond their accomplishments, no matter how impressive. Within each of them lies an essential element which has made them great. I call it the 'inward power' but this is a poor name for the mystery which has baffled philosophers throughout the ages. All I know is that within every man and woman a secret is hidden, and as a photographer it is my task to reveal it if I can. The revelation, if it comes at all, will come in a small fraction of a second with an unconscious gesture, a gleam of the eye, a brief lifting of the mask that all humans wear to conceal their innermost selves from the world. In that fleeting interval of opportunity the photographer must act or lose his prize.'

Acknowledgement is made of courteous permission for quotation of passages from "'That's Georgia'" by Anita Pollitzer, in *Saturday Review of Literature,* XXXIII (November 4, 1950).

Faces of our Time

Aldrin, Armstrong & Collins
THE CREW OF APOLLO XI

The crew of the spaceship that made the first manned landing on the moon. Edwin E. Aldrin, Jr., was born in Montclair, N. J., in 1930, trained as a pilot in the U.S. Air Force, and served in Korea and Germany; studied astronautics at the Massachusetts Institute of Technology; participated in the Gemini IX and XII missions; served as backup command module pilot for the Apollo XI mission, was later involved with advanced planning of missions for NASA, and then appointed head of the aerospace research pilots' school, Edwards Air Force Base. Neil A. Armstrong was born in Wapakoneta, Ohio, in 1930, received his pilot's license on his sixteenth birthday, served in Korea as a naval aviator before joining NASA as a civilian research pilot; at 10.56 p.m. EDT, July 20, 1969, became the first man to set foot on the moon; in 1970, appointed Deputy Associate Administrator of Aeronautics for NASA in Washington. Michael Collins, born in Italy in 1930, attended the U.S. Military Academy and served as an experimental flight test officer in the U.S. Air Force; took part in Gemini VII and X missions; was command pilot of the Apollo XI flight; in 1970, became Assistant Secretary for Public Affairs, Department of State.

The first men to set foot on the moon were still resting from their historic space voyage when I photographed them at the NASA Manned Spacecraft Center in Texas. They had spent the preceding three weeks in quarantine, as a precaution against any lunar organisms they might have carried back to earth. Now they were in high spirits. Remembering the cautionary signs which had surrounded them, they playfully posted one outside my temporary studio: 'Karsh. No Contamination.' ~ The day I photographed them, my wife and I had risen early in Houston to watch our friend, Dr. Michael E. DeBakey, perform open-heart surgery on a twelve-year-old-boy—a 'blue baby operation.' We had stood by his side in the operating room, completely involved and oblivious of time, until the final suture was in place and the boy's previously blue skin colour turned a healthy pink as blood coursed through his newly-widened heart valves. It was a profound religious experience. During the one-and-a-half hour drive to the NASA installation, neither of us spoke, we were so emotionally drained. ~ On arrival at NASA, later than scheduled, I took Neil Armstrong immediately into the astronaut library which served as my studio. My wife meanwhile described in detail the open-heart operation to Edwin 'Buzz' Aldrin. He listened intently. Aldrin is a remarkable man, blond formality on the outside and underneath a mind as fine-honed as a surgeon's scalpel. Finally, he inquired, 'Do you think Dr. DeBakey would ever let me watch an operation?' The surgeon would feel honoured to be asked, Estrellita replied: John Glenn and Frank Borman had already observed many operations. At this point the three astronauts were the idols of an incredulous world—no request seemed impossible to grant. Aldrin paused for a moment. Then he remarked thoughtfully, 'You know, it's a strange thing. I knew that the moon opened to me. I'm just beginning to realise now that the earth is opening, too!' ~ That afternoon, Neil Armstrong invited us to lunch. He looks very much the boy from small-town Ohio, as American as apple pie, with a frank, open, lopsided grin—but he has a streak of mysticism and a concentrated drive that made the years of training and sacrifice for the moon-shot possible. The following week the Apollo XI crew were to begin their first goodwill world tour. During lunch, he kept asking, 'Tell me all about England. Tell me all about France—about Italy—about Africa—about Russia.' Finally we said, 'But you have just been to the moon! Why are you so interested in these mundane places?' Armstrong fixed his searching eyes on us and explained, 'To tell you the truth, that is the only place I've been to!' ~ Michael Collins' early years in a European diplomatic environment had given him an easy social grace and presence. I sensed that, for him, life was more than Apollo. ~ After this photograph was made, Collins took a long relief map of the moon and, with mock solemnity, and an exaggerated flourish of his pen, inscribed one of the yet-unnamed craters as 'Karsh Crater.' Later, Armstrong sent us a print of the famous photograph that showed his boot and his footstep in the moondust. On it he wrote: 'That's one small step for a man; one giant leap for mankind,' his first words on the moon, and added, 'with the best wishes of the photographer.'

MICHAEL COLLINS, EDWIN 'BUZZ' ALDRIN, NEIL A. ARMSTRONG

Marian Anderson

One of the world's leading contraltos. She was born in Philadelphia and as a child sang in her Baptist church choir. A fund raised through a church concert enabled her to take singing lessons under an Italian teacher. In 1925 came public recognition of her talent, when out of 300 she won first prize in a competition in New York. During the next forty years she made many concert tours in the United States and Europe. She gave her farewell concert at Carnegie Hall, New York, in April, 1965. Appointed member of the United States delegation to the United Nations and a member of the U.N. Trusteeship Committee, 1958. U.S. Presidential Medal of Freedom, 1962.

The world knows the voice of Marian Anderson. It has enriched our music, and through it has been made eloquent the long tragedy of the Negro race and her own triumph over it. ~ This realization is for all who hear and see her. What struck me most, however, when I photographed her at her home in Connecticut in 1945, was her simplicity and peacefulness. With her, I was convinced, the harmony of music came from the harmony of her being. The Negro spirituals which have deeply moved us all are not merely the result of a glorious voice and long technical training; they utter her own nature. ~ My problem was to capture and register this quality —not an easy problem even when she fell in with my suggestions with almost childlike obedience. None of my early shots satisfied me in the least. All of them, I felt, had missed the intangible target. I began to despair. Then, towards the conclusion of the sitting, Miss Anderson's accompanist came in for a rehearsal. This seemed to be my chance. I asked him, in a whisper, to play very softly the accompaniment to 'The Crucifixion,' one of the singer's favourite compositions. Unaware of my innocent little plot, she began to hum to herself. Hurriedly, I snapped the camera. When I developed and printed the film I felt that it contained what I had seen with my own eyes. This is the portrait of a harmonious soul revealing itself unconsciously in song. ~ Later, this picture was exhibited at the Museum of Modern Art in New York. A man who saw it there told me afterwards that it had brought tears to his eyes because he remembered his own moving experience with Miss Anderson. He had been one of eleven people invited to her birthday party at her home, 'Mariana Farm,' in Connecticut. Before the guests partook of a light meal, her mother suggested to Miss Anderson that she sing 'The Lord's Prayer.' 'We always say grace before a meal,' the mother explained. As the daughter sang grace that day there were few dry eyes among her listeners. ~ I could understand this after I had studied the Negro singer for myself. She speaks to us, above the clash of race, in the language of all humanity.

Joan Baez

Folk singer and recording artist. Born 1941. Made a modest start singing in coffee houses in Boston. Her international reputation dates from the Newport (Rhode Island) Folk Festival in 1959. Is active in non-violent protest against war and injustice, and is vice-president of the Institute for the Study of Nonviolence, Carmel Valley. In 1968 she published an autobiographical volume, *Daybreak.*

This gifted young American folk singer had eclipsed her original early fame as a long-haired artist of the coffee houses by the time I met her in 1970. She was married with a young child, awaiting the release from prison of her husband, David Harris, who was serving a sentence for draft resistance. She had cheerfully exchanged a life of luxury for her husband's modest home on a bluff near Palo Alto. ~ The day of our photographic session proved a difficult one for her. There was student unrest, with the possibility of riots, on the Stanford University campus. That morning, and the previous one, she had risen early and spent hours at Stanford trying to calm tempers and keep the situation from exploding; the students loved and respected her; her words did much to restore reason. Joan Baez is herself a protester against injustice and war, but a non-violent one. ~ When we first met, she looked exceedingly tired. The exacting and anxious hours with the angry students had taken their toll. Offering me a glass of wine, she asked wistfully, 'Mr. Karsh, would you please let me have a little rest before we start?' Before I knew it, she was sound asleep, curled up like a child in a massive leather chair. Only then did I fully realise how exhausted and drained she was, physically and emotionally. ~ While she slept, I went for a walk in that happy location overlooking San Francisco Bay. As soon as she awakened, she announced brightly, 'Now I am ready for the photograph.' 'No, no,' I replied, 'not yet. You have to shower first, refresh yourself; let us listen to some music and let us talk. *Then* we can settle down to photography.' ~ I picked a cluster of lilac from a flowering bush outside her house and brought it for her to hold; it complemented the mood of serenity which enveloped her. I felt she found the inner strength to carry on from her firm conviction that what her husband was doing was right. Between breaks, and during photography, she cuddled her infant son and sang to him. While we were working she played her records, so that her child would continue to hear his mother's voice. Of all the performers I have photographed, she was the most natural. ~ I photographed her and several other members of the youthful counter-establishment for *Look* magazine. Among these under-thirty personalities, it was re-affirmed to me that people of achievement can be of any age. While they were young in years, there was about each a deep sense of responsibility and concern and response to the world which no longer fit the old stereotype of youthfulness.

JOAN BAEZ

Christiaan Barnard

South African pioneer in heart surgery. Born in Cape Province in 1922; studied medicine and interned in Cape Town. After general practice and further hospital experience there, won the Charles Adams Memorial Scholarship at the University of Minnesota, where he concentrated on cardiothoracic surgery. On his return to South Africa, he specialized in cardiac research and open-heart operations, and performed the first successful open-heart operation in that country. In 1967 he performed the first successful heart transplant from one human to another.

The 'Columbus' of the heart transplant, Dr. Christiaan Barnard, was in Montreal in 1969 for the Second World Conference on Heart Transplantation, chaired by the eminent Canadian cardiovascular surgeon, Dr. Pierre Grondin. Barnard was to address some hundred of his colleagues from all over the world who had performed, or had participated in, a heart transplant operation. To see so many great surgeons gathered together was to me, who had wanted to be a doctor in my youth, a most thrilling experience. My medical-writer wife, who had attended many scientific conferences, gleefully remarked that such a glamorous assemblage was the 'grand opera of medicine, the triumphal procession in the second act of *Aida*, with much pageantry, and horses and camels on the stage.' ~ Christiaan Barnard's single, dramatic operation had brought the world face-to-face with a whole series of ethical considerations. Now that the heart, in literature and in lore (even if not in fact) the repository of the deepest human emotions, could be moved from one body to another, there were new moral issues to be pondered. When should a person be considered technically 'dead'? What is the relationship of donor to recipient? Lay concern with these matters was so great that one of the Oriental transplant surgeons was under indictment for murder and would stand trial when he returned to his own country. ~ One earlier heart transplant had been tried on a chimpanzee; other organs—notably the kidney—had been successfully transferred from one person to another. The heart transplant technique itself was not new: the actual procedure had been perfected in the United States by Drs. Shumway and Lower. But Barnard was the first to carry it out. And because he did it in an obscure hospital in South Africa, because of the special emotional connotations of the heart, because Barnard himself was poor, unknown, and good-looking, the world's attention, fanned by a near-hysterical press, was focused on him. ~ After the initial notoriety, the question facing Barnard was: What now? What happens thereafter to 'Columbus'? After reaching the history books, how does he live the rest of his life? ~ Barnard chose to adopt the clothes and life style of his new jet-set friends. He was constantly in the company of young, beautiful women. Yet, in the midst of all the celebrity-seekers, he never lost the companionship or moral support of his younger brother, Marius, also a surgeon, who had always cared for him. Indeed, Marius had prepared the donor heart for that first history-making operation and handed it to him almost worshipfully. ~ As we were driving to the Montreal Heart Institute, where the photography was to take place, Barnard's new sophistication peeled briefly away. He talked about his dream for a Christiaan Barnard Foundation, to which he was donating all the proceeds from his autobiography, *One Life*. The money would be used to provide transportation and extra care so that needy patients could come to him. When he talked about sick children, and the special surgical challenges of children's cardiovascular diseases, his whole manner changed. The jet-set patter disappeared. The superficial veneer of his personality dropped away. He was once again an enthusiastic physician, imbued with the wonder of what could happen in the operating room—and his role in helping to make it happen.

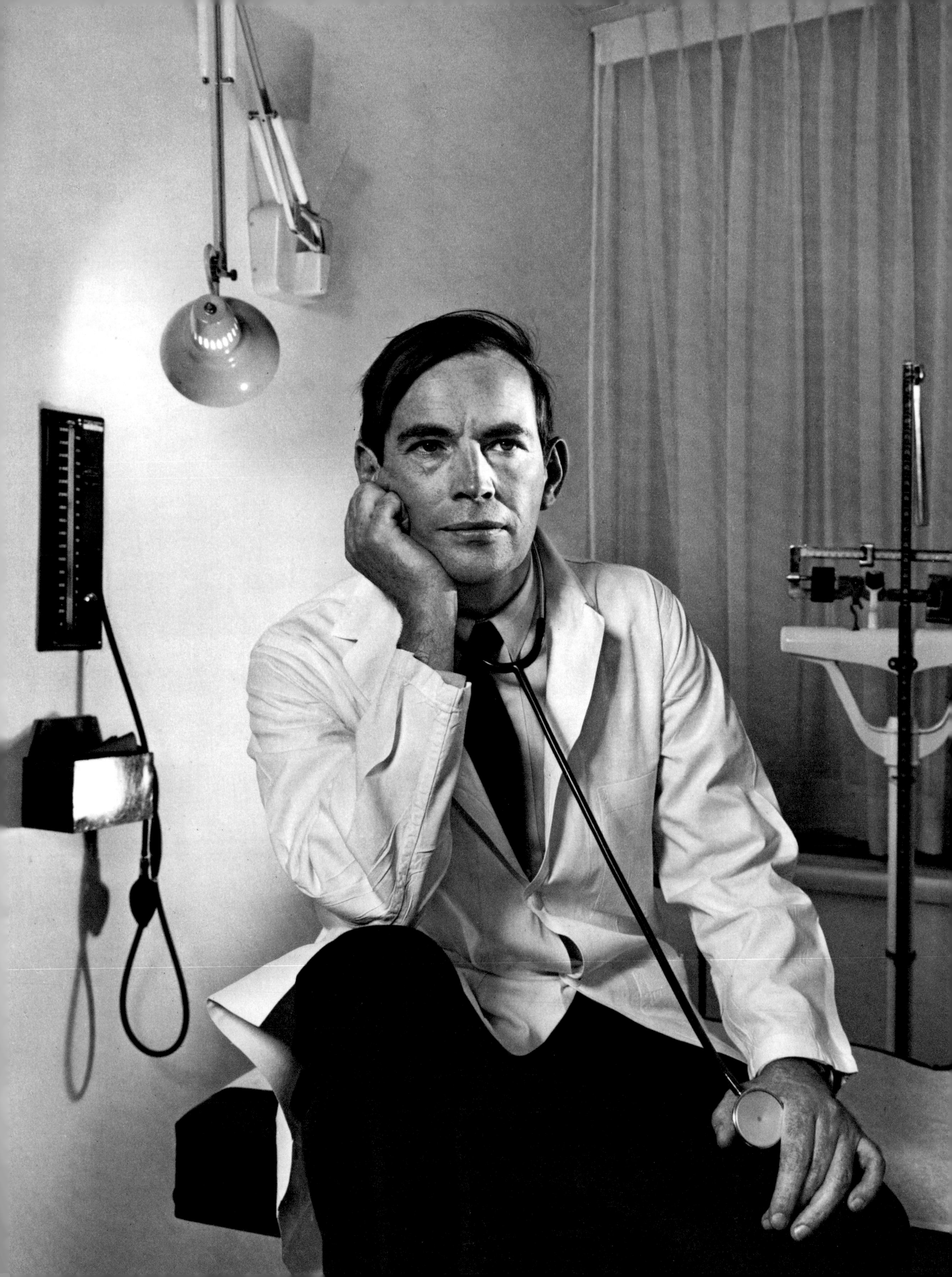

Pablo Casals

World's most celebrated violoncellist, and a composer and conductor. Born in Catalonia, Spain, in 1876 and educated at the Municipal School of Music, Barcelona, and the Madrid Conservatoire. Made his début in England in 1898; conductor of the Pau Casals Symphony Orchestra in Barcelona which he founded. In 1940 he left Spain in protest against the Franco régime and shortly after settled at Prades on the French side of the Pyrenees; since 1950 has conducted there an annual Music Festival which is attended by many famous musicians. In 1956 he moved to San Juan, Puerto Rico, where he inaugurated a second annual Casals Festival of Music. (This portrait was awarded a Gold Medal by the Union of Polish Art Photographers in 1966.)

As I drove along the dusty road to Prades in 1954, I had the feeling that I was on pilgrimage bent. I was going to meet that great self-exile and patron saint of music, Pablo Casals. He did not disappoint me. I had never photographed a warmer or more sensitive human being. ~ We decided to take the portraits in two sessions and against two different backgrounds. The second day we moved to the old Abbey of St. Michel de Cuxa. Though partially restored, it was empty and dark. One electric light bulb was the only illumination available but happily I secured enough current for my strobe lights. No need to pose Casals. Once he had sat down with his cello, the immediate surroundings seemed to fade from his consciousness. Soon the old abbey was throbbing with the music only he can play—music of an almost unearthly quality in this dismal chamber. I hardly dared to talk or move for fear of breaking the spell. And then, as I watched the lonely figure crouched against the rough stones, a small window high above him giving this scene the look of a prison, I suddenly decided on an unusual experiment. I would photograph the musician's back. I would record, if I could, my own vivid impression of the voluntary prisoner who, on the surge of his music, had escaped not only the prison but the world. The portrait printed here perhaps suggests the immense strength, intellectual, physical and spiritual, flowing from this amazing old man. ~ After the sitting I gently returned Casals, his cello and his chair, to his exceedingly small home (really the porter's lodge of an estate) where he invited me into his study for sherry and biscuits. So far as I could see, he had only one frailty in his eightieth year. The sun, or strong light, he said, gave him terrible headaches, and he never went about without his faded red umbrella. ~ I asked him to name the great living composers. 'Very difficult to say,' he replied, 'for me, perhaps Bloch, Enesco and Salazar.' Would any contemporary composer in years to come rank with the classical figures of music? 'I don't know,' he said, 'but I don't believe there is such a genius alive today. For me, classical music is to be adopted, felt, recognized and loved. Modern music has turned towards non-music. Though they have a natural understanding of music, the moderns reject the classical approach as pompous and irrelevant to our time. I hope music will become music again as it has been for centuries from Palestrina to Fauré, Ravel and Debussy.' ~ We toasted each other's health in a last glass of sherry and I departed, with profound sadness and yet elation. The old man waved from the window until my car had disappeared from sight.

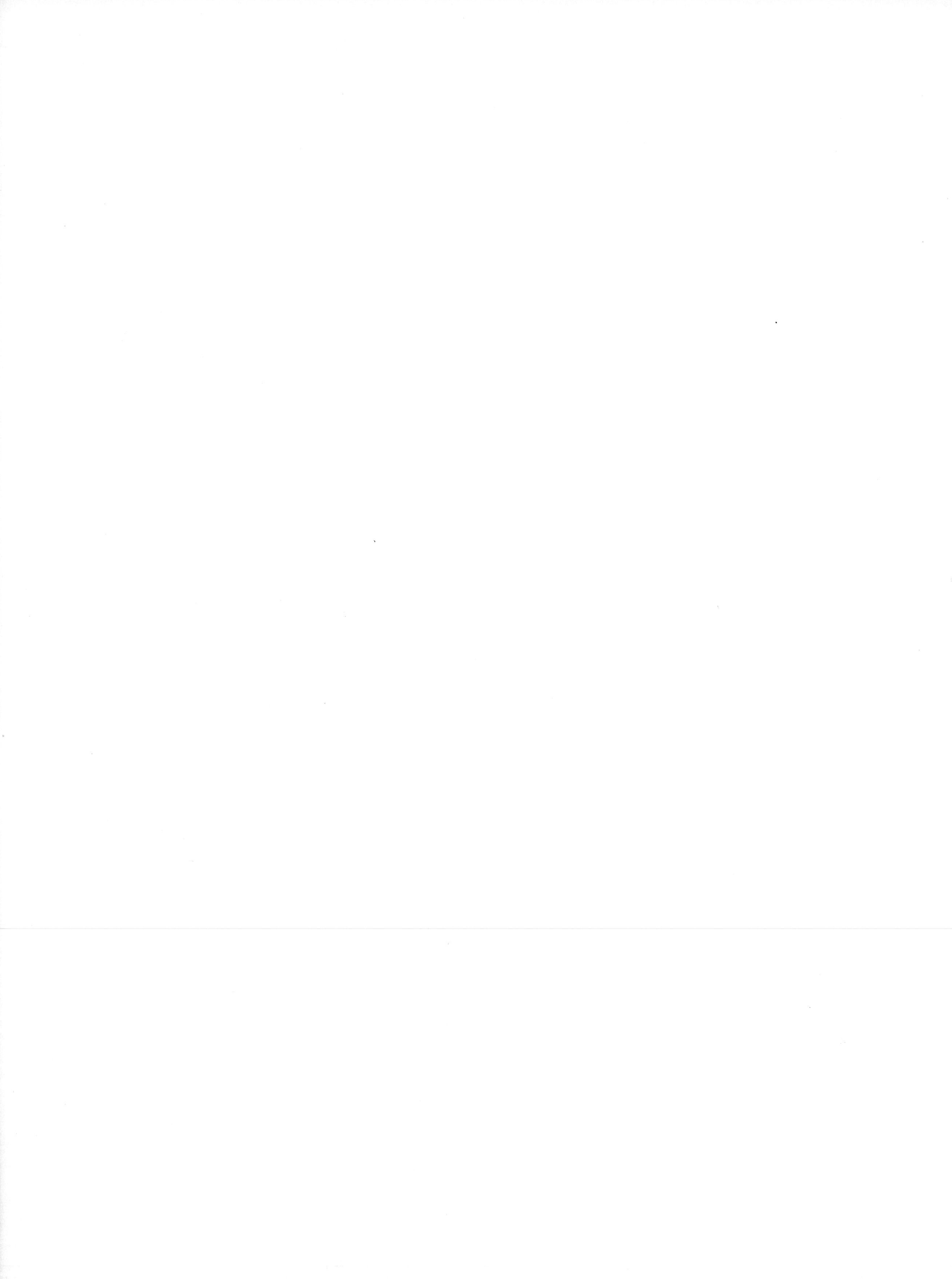

Marc Chagall

Artist, best known for the fanciful, dream-like images of his paintings. Born in 1887 in Vitebsk, Russia, and grew up in a Hasidic Jewish community. Went to Paris to study in 1910 and since then, apart from eight years back in Russia and seven in the United States, has lived in France. Works include engravings, murals, costumes and decor for ballet and theatre, ceramics and stained glass. In 1964 he completed a new ceiling for the Paris Opera. His home is at Vence, northwest of Nice.

When a Parisian concierge speaks well of a tenant, it is an event worth noting. The middle-aged woman who opened the street door of Marc Chagall's apartment building seemed entirely typical of her much-abused class. I asked for the great painter, expecting at best a perfunctory gesture towards his rooms. Instead, she broke into a warm smile and praise. Obviously she loved him. ~ Chagall lives, when he is in Paris, in a romantic old building on the Left Bank, overlooking the Seine. His studio is on the third floor; the steps to it are worn, and there are Gothic madonnas in a niche on the stairwell. The studio was neat, almost compulsively so. Along one wall stood a screen on which he had painted a pair of flying lovers. ~ Chagall was very affable but it seemed to me that, at times, he was playing a role, that of the naive, childlike figure usually portrayed in his public image. Often he referred to himself in the third person—'Chagall did this' —as if he were standing off and looking at himself. It was not an arrogant way of speaking. He gave the impression of a soft and gentle, yet very strong, personality. ~ With his wife, Vava, he had just returned from America where he had been commissioned to paint the murals for the new Metropolitan Opera House. While they were in New York, *Fiddler on the Roof,* a musical based on the life of the Jews in Czarist Russia, was enjoying a great success on Broadway. Had he seen it? No, they had refused many invitations. Any theatrical presentation so close to the circumstances of his own early life in Vitebsk could be nothing, he felt, but a dreadful sham. ~ My assistant at the time was a charming, handsome young Frenchman named Felix Gilbert. At one point Felix had to kneel in front of Chagall to adjust the lights and Chagall, very gently, almost in benediction, placed his hand on the boy's glorious shock of hair and asked, 'Quel âge as-tu?' Felix replied, 'Twenty-seven.' 'Oh,' said Chagall, characteristically placing his hand over his heart, 'to be young!' Just then we heard children coming home from school, and Chagall said, 'You know, when I was a boy in Vitebsk, whenever I wanted to laugh my mother would put her hand over my mouth and say, 'Shah! Shah! Not too loud or *they* might come and get you.' I could never laugh out loud. Now, when I hear children shouting and happy I thank God every day.' He said it without affectation or false piety: God and he were very good friends who understood each other, two cronies sitting down and drinking their glasses of tea together. 'I thank God every day that I can hear such free laughter and I rejoice that these children do not feel the hand of fear clutching at their hearts.' ~ It was good to hear him laugh. And good to know that his laughter, as well as his tears, are permanently recorded on canvas for later generations to see.

The Rt. Hon. Sir Winston Churchill

K.G., P.C., O.M., C.H.

Prime Minister of England 1940–5 and 1951–5, historian and artist. Born 1874; descendant of the Duke of Marlborough; son of Lord Randolph Churchill. His mother, Jennie Jerome, was American, and in 1963 he was made an honorary U.S. citizen by Act of Congress. Educated at Harrow and Sandhurst. Went into the Army in 1895, served in Boer War and in World War I. Entered Parliament in 1900 as Conservative; belonged to Liberal party, 1906–24, then rejoined Conservatives. Member of the House from 1900 and holder of many ministerial posts. Fiercely opposed Conservative Prime Minister Neville Chamberlain's policy of appeasement towards Nazi Germany. He died in 1965. This photograph has appeared on stamps of six nations.

As a private citizen I approached Winston Churchill in 1941 with awe. He was more than the Great Man of the twentieth century; he was even more than an institution. He has become, and will always remain, a gigantic passage in human history. But as a photographer I had a job to be done and it must be done far too fast. ~ Mr. Churchill, as he was then, had been addressing the Canadian Parliament in Ottawa on December 30; he was in no mood for portraiture and two minutes were all he would allow me as he passed from the House of Commons Chamber to an ante-room—two niggardly minutes in which I must try to put on film a man who had already written or inspired a library of books, baffled all his biographers, filled the world with his fame, and me, on this occasion, with dread. ~ He marched in scowling, and regarded my camera as he might regard the German enemy. His expression suited me perfectly, if I could capture it, but the cigar thrust between his teeth seemed somehow incompatible with such a solemn and formal occasion. Instinctively I removed the cigar. At this the Churchillian scowl deepened, the head was thrust forward belligerently, and the hand placed on the hip in an attitude of anger. So he stands in my portrait in what has always seemed to me the image of England in those years, defiant and unconquerable. ~ With a swift change of mood, he came towards me when I was finished, extending his hand and saying, 'Well, you can certainly make a roaring lion stand still to be photographed.'

Michael E. DeBakey

American surgeon. Performed the first implant of an artificial heart in man, April 1966. Educated at Tulane University, New Orleans, and later Associate Professor of Surgery there. During World War II was Director of the Surgical Consultant Division, Office of the Surgeon-General, and in 1946 became U.S. Army Surgical Consultant to the Surgeon-General. Since 1948 has been Professor of Surgery, Baylor College of Medicine, Houston, Texas. He is Director of the Cardiovascular Research Center at the Methodist Hospital in Houston and consultant surgeon to many Texas hospitals. Has served on many national advisory committees and became Chairman of the President's Commission on Heart Disease, Cancer and Stroke in 1964. Numerous awards and honorary degrees, including the U.S. Presidential Medal of Freedom.

'Photograph me at the hospital—the hospital is my life.' So responded Dr. Michael E. DeBakey by telephone from the Methodist Hospital in Houston, Texas. But first came an unexpected opportunity to watch the pioneer of cardiovascular surgery at work. Wrapped in sterile green surgical cap and gown, my wife and I stood close beside his elbow in the operating theatre. ~ The emergency operation was for an aneurysm of the aorta, a surgical technique DeBakey had pioneered in the mid-fifties. As we watched, the aneurysm—a bulging, diseased section of the large artery leading from the heart—was cut away and replaced with a nylon implant. ~ Even surrounded by his team of assistants, nurses, and anaesthesiologists, Dr. DeBakey seemed enclosed in his own circle of self-containment—involved, yet very much alone. In this microcosm of life and death, he was the undisputed master. His slight, wiry figure dominated the operating room with enormous power of concentration. ~ His surgical assistant that day was not attuned to him: there was a slight time lag in response. DeBakey became irritable and impatient. He used the suction himself. He reached for an instrument from the table nearby; he even bent the retractor to the desired angle, his every gesture urging more perfect co-ordination. I watched entranced at his quest for perfection, and understood so well his frustration when it was not forthcoming. I turned to my wife and whispered, 'He is marvellous—so intolerant, so impatient—just like me!' ~ In the midst of his intense concern for his patient, DeBakey turned to us and asked, 'Are you sure you can see everything? Come closer, I want you to watch the suturing.' We looked down into the exposed heart as DeBakey stitched the ends of the patient's aorta onto the nylon implant, ever so delicately, his sensitive fingers moving eloquently with assured mastery, yet reverently as instruments in extending life. ~ This crucial part of the operation over, he left the operating room. For a few seconds his dynamism kept the tension at the same high pitch, then everyone noticeably relaxed. ~ The following day, before we began our photographic session, I inquired anxiously, 'How is our patient?' He was doing fine. Without the operation, he might have lived perhaps twenty-four hours before his diseased aorta 'blew.' Now he could soon resume a normal life. ~ As we worked, we talked of DeBakey's other interests: music, fine craftsmanship, photography, all of which, regrettably, he no longer pursues. He dedicates all his time to the advancement of cardiovascular surgery and research, lecturing, teaching, operating. 'Participation in the exciting world of inquiry and discovery is, in fact, its own reward,' he remarked. ~ Our hours together were marked by mutual understanding and relaxation rare, I am sure, in either of our professional lives. We discussed the Golden Rule, which DeBakey thinks especially applicable to medicine: 'A good scientist is, in fact, first a humanist and second a scientist.' In reply to my questions about experimentation in medicine, DeBakey reaffirmed, 'Above all, the researcher must preserve a humane approach to science.' ~ He then left to catch an afternoon plane to speak in New York, on yet another leg of his driven, ceaseless journey in pursuit of his calling.

M.E.D.

Albert Einstein

Physicist; discoverer and exponent of the theory of relativity. Born in Switzerland in 1879 and died in the United States in 1955. After holding appointments at the Universities of Zurich and Prague, he was appointed Professor of Physics at Berlin University and Director of the Kaiser Wilhelm Institute for Physics in 1914; he became a German citizen. He renounced this citizenship and his appointment in 1933, left Europe for the United States, and was made a member for life of the Institute for Advanced Study at Princeton. In 1940 he became an American citizen. During World War II he did research work on explosives for the United States Navy.

Among the tasks that life as a photographer had set me, a portrait of Albert Einstein had always seemed a 'must'—not only because this greatest refugee of our century has been accounted by all the world (except his homeland) as the outstanding scientist since Newton, but because his face, in all its rough grandeur, invited and challenged the camera. ~ When I saw him for the first time at Princeton University's Institute for Advanced Study, in February 1948, I found exactly what I had expected—a simple, kindly, almost childlike man, too great for any of the tricks or postures of eminence. Yet one did not have to understand his science to feel at once the power of his mind. ~ Awed before this unique intellect, I yet ventured to ask Einstein his views on human immortality. He mused for a moment and then replied: 'What I believe of immortality? There are two kinds. The first lives in the imagination of people and is thus an illusion. There is a relative immortality which may conserve the memory of an individual for some generations. But there is only one true immortality, on a cosmic scale, and that is the immortality of the cosmos itself. There is no other.' ~ He spoke of these ultimate mysteries as calmly as he might answer a student's question about mathematics—with such an air of quiet confidence, indeed, that I found his answer profoundly disturbing to one who held other views. I turned the conversation, and knowing him to be an accomplished violinist, asked if there were any connection between music and mathematics. 'In art,' he said, 'and in the higher ranges of science, there is a feeling of harmony which underlies all endeavour. There is no true greatness in art or science without that sense of harmony. He who lacks it can never be more than a great technician in either field.' ~ Was he optimistic about the future harmony of mankind itself? He appeared to ponder deeply and remarked in graver tones: 'Optimistic? No. But if mankind fails to find a harmonious solution then there will be disaster on a dimension beyond anyone's imagination.' To what source should we look for the hope of the world's future? 'To ourselves,' said Einstein. ~ He spoke sadly yet serenely, as one who had looked into the universe far past mankind's small affairs. In this humour my camera caught him . . . the portrait of a man beyond hope or despair.

Elizabeth the Second

By the Grace of God, of the United Kingdom
of Great Britain and Northern Ireland and
of her other realms and territories, Queen,
Head of the Commonwealth, Defender of the Faith

H.R.H. The Prince Philip, Duke of Edinburgh

Prince of the United Kingdom of Great Britain
and Northern Ireland, Earl of Merioneth,
Baron Greenwich of Greenwich in the
County of London, K.G., K.T.

Robert Frost

American poet. Born in San Francisco, 1874; died in Boston, 1963. Father died when poet was ten and he moved with his mother to New England, the usual background for his poems. Studied at Dartmouth College and Harvard University; worked as bobbin-boy, editor, farmer, teacher of psychology. Trip to England, 1912, marked beginning of his career as a poet; in 1913 *A Boy's Will* was published in London and hailed by English poets, including Rupert Brooks and Lascelles Abercrombie. Professor of English at Amherst College, 1916–20, 1923–5, 1926–38, 1949–63; 'poet in residence' at the University of Michigan, 1921–3; Emerson Fellow at Harvard University, 1939–43; Resident Consultant in Humanities, Dartmouth College, 1943–9; appointed Consultant in the Humanities to the Library of Congress, 1959. Helped to found the Breadloaf School at Middlebury College, 1920, and returned every summer as a lecturer. Pulitzer Prize winner in 1924, 1931, 1937, 1943. His works include: *A Boy's Will, North of Boston, A Witness Tree, Aforesaid.* He recited his poem *The Gift Outright* at the inauguration of President John F. Kennedy, January 1961.

'Don't make a saint of me,' said Mr. Frost as he faced my camera in 1958. 'I'm a rascal. Why, they call me Scarface Frost from Chicago.' This was my introduction to the crusty, beloved American poet, an old man who did precisely as he pleased. At the time he was sitting in his littered, chaotic studio at Cambridge, Massachusetts. There he worked at what he was pleased to call his desk—a dilapidated piece of Ten-Test supported by a piece of string and a battered walking stick. Yet, I thought, out of all this bedlam comes so much beauty. ~ Some of that native, homely American candour for which he is famous began to appear as we went to work. His mind moved suddenly from one subject to another in long leaps. 'Painting, sculpture, and photography,' he commented, 'may be international but poetry is a medium for the nationalists. The thought may be universal, but the expression of it is nationalistic. I have never seen an instance when one of my poems was translated into a foreign language without losing the idiom of the original.' ~ Then he remembered that T. S. Eliot had once asked him what he meant by the expression, 'Good fences make good neighbours.' Although Frost had not invented that phrase (it was a folk-saying from New England), he was not surprised that Eliot should object to it. 'Eliot's characters,' Mr. Frost said, 'never know boundaries, not even of each other's beds.' ~ He recalled his recent visit to the United Nations in New York, where he had been taken to the Meditation Room. The only symbol there was of pure iron—a symbol of man's strength and unity. At this Frost scoffed and instantly composed a new, derisive couplet to decorate the shrine. He recited it to me: 'Nature within her inmost self divides To trouble men with having to take sides.' ~ 'Those silly people down there,' he said, 'talking about love all the time! They make me hate. You only value one when it's offset by the other. You always have victory and defeat, good and evil, love and hate, God and the devil.' ~ I asked him about his way of writing a poem. He said it was like making a witticism… it just came. 'And,' he added, 'it only comes fifteen or twenty times a year.' ~ Mr. Frost talked at length about his lectures, explaining that he would rather make a speech than read his poetry; every poem says all he had to say on that subject. When I told him that I would come to his next lecture in order to ask him questions, he said, 'Hmph, you will be the only one that does.'

Yuri Alexeyevich Gagarin

Soviet Air Force officer and cosmonaut; first man to enter space, April 12, 1961, on an orbital flight in the spaceship *Vostok.* Killed in testflight crash, March 1968. Born 1934 in family of a collective farmer in the Smolensk region of Russia. Educated as foundry worker. While at technical school, joined Saratov Aero-Club and later entered the Air Force school; graduated as Grade A pilot in 1957. Member of the Communist Party of the Soviet Union. Deputy to Supreme Soviet, U.S.S.R.; President, Soviet-Cuba Friendship Society. Joined staff of Zhukovsky Air Force Academy, 1961.

Space pioneers in the Soviet Union are truly popular heroes: a man would have to be both astronaut and movie star to be equally idolized in North America. Public adulation reaches its peak each year at the anniversary of man's first venture beyond the earth. On April 12, the cosmonauts are swept along a continuous round of functions. They take the salute at Lenin's Tomb, they are interviewed, they make speeches, they are entertained. Every minute is occupied. It was on this day of days that I photographed them in 1963. ~ We were to meet Gagarin, and the three other men who had, by that time, followed him through space, in an old mansion close to Red Square, the home of the USSR–Canada Friendship Society. My cameras and lights were set up in a large room crowded with people also waiting to see Russia's idols. Although it was mid-afternoon, the cosmonauts had been allowed no break for lunch. They could stop here only a few minutes. I had not taken portraits under such pressure since wartime, and I thought those days had passed. ~ At 3.30 they arrived, Gagarin coming first. As I saw him approaching down a long corridor, I was reminded immediately by his walk, and by his very open and spontaneous smile, of the popular General Eisenhower who came back from Europe in the 1940's. He wore the uniform of a lieutenant-colonel, and only a few decorations—his first-class pilot's wings, the flag-like badge of a member of the Supreme Soviet, the five-sided emblem reserved for cosmonauts, the star of a Hero of the Soviet Union. He was rather withdrawn, modest and shy. All four of the cosmonauts were splendid men, very polite and helpful, delighted by the adulation, but their heads obviously not turned by it. ~ There was no chance to talk with them. One of the very few questions was put, not by me, but by our translator. Until then that young lady had been very blasé about the famous men and women we had been meeting. But on this day she appeared in a new blouse, with her hair and nails freshly done, and as soon as she had a chance she asked Andriyan Nikolayev, the one unmarried cosmonaut (who eventually married Valentina Tereshkova, the first woman space traveller), 'Is there a wedding in the offing?' It was the first time she had ever spoken on her own, and really she was asking, 'Are you still available?' Which goes to show that women are women wherever you may go.

ВЕРХОВНЫЙ
СОВЕТ
СССР

Alberto Giacometti

Swiss sculptor, painter, and poet. Born 1901. Studied in Geneva and in Italy, then settled in Paris, where by the late 1920s he had become associated with the surrealist movement. He began to produce the elongated, solitary figures for which he is largely known after an illness in 1945. Works are on exhibition in Baltimore Museum of Art, Museum of Modern Art in New York, Tate Gallery in London, and in principal museums of modern art in France, Switzerland, and Italy, and figure in many private collections. He died in 1966.

My experience with Giacometti began with a surprise. He was still asleep when we arrived at his studio, in a working-class district in Paris, at the agreed-upon hour of three in the afternoon. The sculptor and his brother, Diego, who was Giacometti's favourite and most constant model, had shared that same studio for 38 years, since leaving their native Switzerland. Diego still continued to paint exquisite custom-made lamps for exclusive Parisian interior decorators—a task which had also occupied Alberto before his sculpture began to sell. I did not know then that three in the afternoon was Giacometti's usual breakfast hour, and that he usually worked through the night. ~ I urged him to go to his neighbourhood bistro for coffee, so that I could have time to set up my equipment in the unbelievably cluttered, tiny room which served as his atelier. All around, in semi-darkness and dirt, were his characteristic elongated figures, many still uncast, in clay. They dominated the room; they pervaded the atmosphere. ~ My wife could stand it only a short time before she rushed out to the welcome release of the open air. She told me afterward that, while she enjoyed Giacometti's attenuated figures in a museum full of light and space, to experience the sculptures in the crowded atelier was a far different matter. She felt as if she were in unredeemable hell—that here was a place without grace, without hope, without humour, without redemption—that she was among the living dead—and she grieved for the tortured sensibility which had produced this. And what, by some symbolic twist, did she discover when she was out under the blue sky again? That the building next door was a clinic for expectant mothers and new babies, so that just two feet away from this site of horror was new life. ~ Giacometti was still in an uncertain temper when he returned. He could not sit still for a moment; he stamped his foot impatiently like a child; he smoked constantly. His face was ashen grey and he did not welcome any conversation which might bring a ray of communicative humour into the afternoon. My experience should have prepared me to realise he was in excruciating pain. ~ Soon after, when his spasm of agony somewhat subsided, he invited me to a lengthy visit with him and his New York dealer, Pierre Matisse, the son of the great French artist. We stood in the alleyway outside the studio, the passage so narrow we could touch both walls of the adjacent buildings with our fingertips, and reality seemed to right itself again, as we discussed the current art scene. ~ That same evening, when my wife and I were with our friend, the painter Jean-Paul Riopelle, at La Coupole, the famous rendezvous for artists in Montparnasse, Giacometti and a companion came in. He greeted us wistfully and put his gnarled hand on my shoulder and said to me in French, 'I know I was a bad boy this afternoon; I didn't mean it. Forgive me.' In the amber half-light of the cafe, my wife observed the craggy planes of his face as he leaned forward to listen intently to his companion; it was tormented, yet concerned and gentle. A few weeks later, he was dead.

Martha Graham

American dancer and choreographer. Born in Pittsburgh, 1902; studied at Denishaw School of Dancing, Los Angeles, where she was later a student-teacher. Made her first independent appearance in a dance recital, 1926; founded Dance Repertory Theatre in New York, 1930, and subsequently established Martha Graham School of Contemporary Dance in New York. Among her works: *Primitive Mysteries, El Penitente, Errand into the Maze, Letter to the World,* and *Appalachian Spring*. Also, together with Agnes de Mille, has provided dances for *Oklahoma* and *Carousel; One Touch of Venus* and *Finian's Rainbow* included examples of Miss Graham's work. Capegio Award, 1959; Aspen Award in the Humanities, 1965.

As everybody knows, Martha Graham has originated, out of the dance, a new art form. Naturally, I wished to photograph her in the posture and mood of the dance. But this seemed impossible under the circumstances. Upon arriving at Miss Graham's New York apartment in 1948 I was quite taken aback, though impressed, by the stark simplicity with which she had chosen to surround herself. On a modernistic table stood a grotesque piece of petrified wood, vaguely suggesting the attitude of a modern dancer. A rubber plant in one corner, a few pieces of very modern furniture, no pictures, no radio, no decorations of any sort—this, then, was to be the setting of a dancer's portrait. Then I looked up to the ceiling and it seemed only a few inches above my head. No one, not even Martha Graham, could dance in such a place. ~ Compromise sometimes must be the stuff of which pictures are made. So, rather hopelessly, I sat Miss Graham on a low stool and asked her to assume various attitudes as if she had the space of a great stage around her. Amazingly enough, this restricted posture presented no problem, such perfect control had she over her body. She was sitting on a stool, in a low room, but she seemed to be dancing. In fact, she was dancing, and thus I recorded her. ~ She talked to me about the dance but clearly with a single-minded devotion to her own type of art. Though it has won wide acceptance, she thought it 'went over' with younger people better than with older audiences. 'The young,' she said, 'have an appetite for experiment and experience, which is all that is really necessary. They have the habit of looking inside because of their concentration and study of psychology in schools today.' ~ Martha Graham's new trend in dancing may be labelled impressionistic or given some other name, but it is certainly based on sound choreography. Yet where older dance forms often seem stilted, her dance is fluid and, therefore, it seems to me, more representative of this fluid and changing age. ~ She submerges herself in her work utterly—even under a low ceiling and on a stool—so that she seems mentally and physically apart. Yet her art is never isolated from her audience. Like any art, it is lonely in creation but instantly communicates with all who watch it, as I, in an unlikely setting, watched it.

Ernest Hemingway

American novelist and war correspondent. Born 1898; educated in elementary schools and abroad. Used much of his personal experience in his novels and stories (of World War I in Italy as ambulance driver and soldier; the expatriate society of Paris in the twenties, when he met and was influenced by Ezra Pound and Gertrude Stein; the Spanish civil war, which he covered as newspaper correspondent). War correspondent in China, 1941, and on Western Front. His works include: *The Sun Also Rises, A Farewell to Arms, For Whom the Bell Tolls,* and *The Old Man and the Sea* (Pulitzer Prize, 1953); all these have been made into films. Awarded Nobel Prize for Literature in 1954. He was found dead of a shotgun wound in 1961 in his home at Ketchum, Idaho.

In his books and his stories Ernest Hemingway brought to life a swarming company of characters, but he jealously concealed himself. After reading those tales of ferocity, violence, and physical suffering, I expected to meet in the author a composite image of his creations. Instead, in 1957 at his home near Havana, I found a man of peculiar gentleness, the shyest man I ever photographed. Therein, I imagine, lies the secret of his life and work. He felt in his soul, with lonely anguish, the tragedy of our species and expressed it in his writing, but, for self-protection, built around himself a wall of silence and myth. ~ Nevertheless, I wanted him to talk, to focus his mind, and hence his face, on some subject which would arouse both; so I asked him bluntly what he thought about that large tribe of writers who try to imitate his style. Forgetting his diffidence, he gave me a ready answer. The trouble with the imitators, he said, was that they were able only to pick out the obvious faults in his work; they invariably missed his real purpose and his real method—just as many readers remembered him chiefly for his defects. There was no bitterness in this remark, only a rather sad amusement. ~ As he thought about my question I discovered that he had a wonderful smile—alive, kindly, and full of understanding. But on developing my negatives I liked best the portrait printed here. It is, I think, a true portrait, the face of a giant cruelly battered by life, but invincible. ~ And what an astounding life this man had survived, quite apart from his work! He talked quietly about his airplane accidents. He was still suffering from injuries that would have killed most men. The worst of it was the doctor's strict diet. Perhaps he would soon be allowed more than a few glasses of wine every day. 'I don't drink while I write,' he added. 'You can't write serious stuff and drink.' I suggested that he must be quite unlike Churchill in that respect and he retorted: 'Churchill is a writer of rhetoric and to write rhetoric you must drink. But that's not my trade.' ~ I tried to start him talking of his writing but was not successful. Once he had written a book, he said, it went out of his mind completely and no longer interested him. There must never be any residue from one book carried into another. Every book was a new challenge, I gathered, an experiment and an adventure. 'I must forget what I have written in the past,' he explained, 'before I can project myself into a new work.' ~ As we were leaving, my wife noted some flowers growing between the stone steps of the garden. A gardener herself, she approved of flowers grown in this manner, though they disturbed the stones. 'Yes,' said Hemingway, 'but we can always replace the stones.' Between the rough boulders of this man's prose, I thought, the flowers of compassion will always grow, whether the public notices them or not.

Augustus John
O.M.

British painter (1878–1961). Studied at the Slade School, 1896–9. Taught at Liverpool University Art School; member of New English Art Club; Royal Academician, 1928–38; re-elected 1940. Trustee of the Tate Gallery; President, Society of Mural Painters; President, Royal Society of Portrait Painters. Many of his best known and most important paintings feature gipsy or peasant subjects; he himself spent much time in gipsy encampments. Examples: 'The Mumpers,' 'Galway,' 'The Lyric Fantasy.' Also some major works in field of portraiture: George Bernard Shaw and Dylan Thomas.

The English portrait painter Augustus John may seem somewhat melancholy, grim, and alarming in my portrait. That quality of brooding remoteness is one side of him and no doubt lies close to his genius. But our meeting in 1954 was warm and gay. One of those afternoon teas was served that are the glory of old England, and at it Mr. John's charming wife presided in their Hampshire home. ~ What, I ventured to ask, did he think of portraiture by film as compared to canvas and brush? 'Well, of course,' he said, 'they are quite different media. You can't fairly compare them. Yet both in their own ways are capable of great things. But then, you know that already. You have proved it with your camera.' ~ He made it clear that he had little use for most contemporary painters. The old masters were his idols. Michelangelo, Raphael, Rubens, Rembrandt—he spoke of them with candid idolatry. 'These great men,' he added, 'liked best to portray the common man.' So did John, as his portraits show. When I compared his simple yet powerful drawings to those of the immortals, he stood up suddenly in the middle of our sitting, bowed deeply and, with a comic flourish, announced: 'No greater honour can be paid to any artist.' ~ Luckily I seemed to have said just the right thing to produce the mood of relaxation and rather wistful contemplation that I wanted to record—the look of the man who sees his own private visions of beauty behind the faces of his subjects. At any rate, he was an ideal subject and our time together passed far too quickly. ~ It was getting late and I had to take my leave. At the door Mr. John put his arm around my shoulders and said a little plaintively, 'I wish I could offer you some further hospitality.' Already he had offered me much. But the thing I would remember was the simple integrity of the artist, his devotion to his own ideals of art, a master's loyalty to the artists of the past. He followed his own path and, I think, he followed it alone, quite undisturbed by modern fashion and inwardly happy with his quest.

His Holiness Pope John XXIII

Born Angelo Giuseppe Roncalli in 1881, son of a peasant farmer in Lombardy, North Italy; died, 1963. Studied at seminary in Bergamo; later won scholarship to the Pontifical Seminary, Rome. Ordained, 1904; returned to Lombardy as secretary to Bishop of Bergamo and as a teacher at the seminary. Served as Chaplain in Italian army during World War I. Made an Archbishop, 1925, and given first diplomatic assignment—Apostolic Delegate in Bulgaria; promoted to Nuncio, 1930; sent to Turkey and Greece as Apostolic Delegate, 1934; appointed Nuncio to France, 1944; permanent observer of the Holy See to Unesco, 1952; returned to Italy on being made a Cardinal in 1953 as Patriarch of Venice. Elected Pope in 1958. During his reign the first Vatican Council in nearly a century was summoned.

Having photographed Pope Pius XII and happily produced his favourite portrait, since distributed in millions of copies throughout the world, I was naturally eager to put on film the rugged, manly features of his successor, Pope John XXIII. ~ Once again, however, my task was made more difficult by the fact that His Holiness could spare only a little time from his many duties. Arriving in Rome on December 27, 1958, I was unable to photograph His Holiness until January 2. Meanwhile, however, I was invited to attend a Baciamano (literally, hand-kissing), a ceremony which included only twenty-four persons, in the Hall of Tapestries. We all kissed the Holy Father's ring and he, in turn, had appropriate words for each of us. Then he blessed us from the centre of the room saying 'Let me offer you a collective benediction that you may take it with you and share it with all those you meet in any part of the world.' Afterwards I attended a General Audience in the Clementine Hall where the Pope addressed a large gathering from his throne, with the aid of a microphone, in Italian. I asked one of the nuns what he had talked about and she replied with a smile, 'About his youth.' That same afternoon I found myself in the Hall of Benedictions listening with fascination to Handel's *Messiah* presented by the Opera House of Venice, the city of which Pope John was Archbishop and Patriarch before his election. He was carried to the concert on his sedia and I noted that he had a special word of acknowledgment for his bearers. ~ By this time I had formed a clear and, I think, accurate impression of His Holiness as a compelling personality, a simple, forthright human being, a theologian of genius no doubt, but a man among men and already, I should suppose, a major figure in the long history of his Church, to which he had brought, even at his advanced age, an extraordinary power of leadership, and also of imagination. ~ That impression was confirmed when, after several nights of worry, I arrived at last in his presence and went to work. Speaking in French, I recalled a newspaper headline, 'Le Pape est en prison' (The Pope is in prison). That report, referring to his recent visit to convicts, seemed to amuse him. Then, as the time was ticking away very slowly from the Vatican's point of view, and very swiftly from mine, His Holiness asked me whether I was not tired. 'No, Your Holiness,' I said, 'but very anxious.' So I was, until the portrait was finally printed at my studio in Ottawa. As I left him, he imparted his blessings with a spontaneous, fatherly smile, adding 'Bene, bene, bene.' Placing his hands on my shoulders he said, 'I wish you to enter into your diary that you have had the longest visit with Pope John to date.'

Yasunari Kawabata

Japanese novelist and short-story writer, first Japanese winner of the Nobel Prize in Literature, 1968. Born 1899. Began writing for the student magazine at Tokyo University; later joined the staff of *Bungei Shunjū*, a literary journal, and in 1924 co-founded the avant-garde *Bungei Jidai*. His writing has been influenced by the bereavements he suffered in childhood (by the age of sixteen he had lost his parents, his only sister, and his grandparents) and by traditional Buddhist literature. President of the PEN Club of Japan, 1948–65, and since 1959 Vice-President of the International PEN Club. Among his works best-known in the West are *Snow Country* (1957) and *Thousand Cranes* (1959).

The Japanese have a charming custom: instead of honouring their great men with peerages or knighthoods, they give them the respectful title, 'living human treasure,' that is, a person treasured by the entire nation. Yasunari Kawabata is one such 'human treasure,' the country's outstanding novelist, and the winner of the Nobel Prize for Literature in 1968. I was guided to him when I was in search of prominent Japanese to include in an exhibit of my portraits which toured that country in 1970. ~ We met in Kawabata's home in Kamakura, just behind a great bronze Buddha, near the sea. He had two houses really, a low, sprawling, old one of traditional architecture, and a new wing still under construction that was mostly western in concept. Both stood in a beautiful Japanese garden. The surroundings were eclipsed however by the presence of our serene and gracious host, whose every utterance, every movement, held beauty. One felt his gentle understanding at all times. ~ Had the Nobel Prize, the first to any Japanese author, changed his life in any way? 'No', he replied, 'there is no difference, only that I thoroughly enjoyed the trip to Sweden to receive it.' We asked which of his works was his favourite. 'I am not really satisfied with any,' he answered. ~ After several pictures had been taken, I asked whether he had some work of art that might be included. He said, 'Yes. Yes, I will go and fetch something that will please your eye.' And with much ceremony and tenderness he brought out a square wooden box. Inside it lay a piece of funerary sculpture (*haniwa*) about two millennia old, an earthenware portrait of a child's head with a nose that perfectly echoed Kawabata's own. ~ We knew he had written some much talked-of articles from the Zen viewpoint. Did he think, we asked, that its many western enthusiasts could truly understand Zen? 'How can they thoroughly understand it?' he replied. 'I do not, although because I occasionally write or speak of it people consider me an authority. I only observe it. People see in Zen what they wish to see. Isn't religion a mirror which reflects both the observers and the vision?' ~ He calls himself an observer of life rather than a combatant. Does he have a philosophy? 'Not exactly, I would rather say a sense of beauty, a kind of *maborisi*.' This word means a vision, a phantom, a mirage; the dictionary has no exact translation. 'I have this *maborisi*,' he continued, 'and it makes me pursue beauty.'

Helen Keller

Born in 1880 in Tuscambia, Alabama; died in 1968. As a result of illness she was completely blind and deaf from the age of nineteen months. On behalf of the blind she lectured extensively all over the world and held many awards for her work in relief of the handicapped. Her books include *Helen Keller's Journal* (1938) and *Let Us Have Faith* (1941). Her youthful triumph over handicap was told in the popular play and film, *The Miracle Worker.*

On first looking into the blind but seeing eyes of perhaps the greatest woman in our world, I said to myself: 'The light comes from within.' And what a light of courage shines through the face from the dauntless soul of Helen Keller! ~ Katharine Cornell, her devoted friend, had taken me to Miss Keller's apartment in New York, in 1948, and explained the ritual of our meeting. The woman who has no sight or hearing shook my hand and then placed her marvellously sensitive fingers on my face. In her mind's eye, I knew, she already had me completely photographed. We were *en rapport* and I could make my portrait. Although I could speak to Miss Keller only through Miss Polly Thomson, her faithful companion, who dialled braille into Miss Keller's palm, we soon developed a code of our own. At the slightest pressure of my fingers on her hand, she knew at once exactly which way I wished her to turn and at what angle I wanted her head. Her extreme sensitivity, her alert mind, her kindness and understanding, but most of all her gaiety, kept me amazed throughout the whole sitting. ~ Sight and hearing had passed into her hands. Therefore a portrait of the hands was as important as a portrait of her face—hands that create light out of darkness, sound out of perpetual silence, and alone bring this woman into communion with nature and her own kind. So I photographed those hands and as I looked at the result I repeated my first observation of Miss Keller: the light did indeed come from within. ~ Our sitting finished, I said to her, 'You wouldn't know, but this is not the first time I have met you. One of my earliest attempts to read English, years ago, was an article in the *Reader's Digest* called 'How to Appreciate the Beauties of Sunset.' You wrote it. Now, having met you in person I shall no longer think of you in terms of sunset but of sunrise!' 'How I wish,' she quickly replied, 'that all men would take sunrise for their slogan and leave the shadows of sunset behind them.' That chance remark, it seemed to me, told the story of Helen Keller better than a library of books. By her incredible victory over the flesh she had left the shadows behind her. Blind, she had seen the sunrise; deaf, she had heard the music of the spheres. I left her with a new sense of our human possibilities.

John Fitzgerald Kennedy

35th President of the United States; the youngest man, and the first Roman Catholic, to be elected to that office. Born in 1917 and educated at Harvard University. Served with distinction as commander of a U.S. Navy motor torpedo boat during World War II. Member of the U.S. House of Representatives, 1947–53. U.S. Senator from Massachusetts, 1953–61. Author of *Profiles in Courage,* for which he won the 1957 Pulitzer Prize for biography, and three other books. As Democratic candidate in the 1960 presidential election, he won a narrow victory over Richard M. Nixon. On November 22, 1963, during a visit to Dallas, Texas, he was shot and killed by a sniper.

I photographed John F. Kennedy twice during his campaign in 1960 for the Presidency of the United States. The first time, in August, was with Mrs. Kennedy at the home of her mother, Mrs. Hugh Auchincloss. Working with those two young people was a rare experience. It is always pleasant to photograph a handsome man beside one of the world's most alluring women. They needed no coaching. Between them one sensed a wonderful intuitive understanding. ~ The Senator was under considerable pressure that morning. Several bills of the utmost importance were pending. Every few minutes he would excuse himself to telephone for a progress report, in case he should need to rush off to vote. Yet between these interruptions, during a session which lasted two hours, he seemed completely able to throw off politics. I was enormously impressed by his ability to live in the present, to concentrate completely on the job of the moment. ~ The next time we met was in the Senate offices, where I was to photograph both Kennedy and Lyndon Johnson. The elections were closer now. One might have expected to find the Presidential candidate tired and harassed; but like any thoroughbred he had summoned fresh reserves as the chance of triumph approached. He was thoughtful enough to suggest that instead of my moving my photographic equipment, he would come to Johnson's office. ~ Kennedy had not realized that the pictures would be taken in colour as well as in black and white and considered his necktie unsuitable. 'Well then,' he said, 'let me have yours.' As a result, the portrait on the facing page shows this most meticulous dresser wearing a tie borrowed on the spur of the moment. ~ 'Senator Kennedy,' I asked, 'the constitution allows a President only two terms. Even if you serve for eight years, you will still be a young man in 1968. What will you do then? Do you think an ex-President should be made a Senator for life? Will you write? Will you work for the party?' He replied, 'Those are too many questions to ask at once. Let me reflect a bit.' After a long silence, he said: 'No, I would like to start something altogether different.' ~ At this moment the door opened and Johnson came in. Clasping his hands, Kennedy looked up at his running mate as they discussed some details of campaign strategy. And in retrospect, there is in this attitude a poignant prophetic note. I clicked the shutter, but lost the chance to enquire further into his post-Presidential plans. To the world's tragic loss, there were to be no such years for him.

Nikita Sergeyevich Khrushchev

First Secretary of the Communist Party of the Soviet Union, 1953–64, and Chairman of the Council of Ministers of the U.S.S.R. (Prime Minister), 1958–64. Born 1894. Joined the Communist Party in 1918 and was active in Moscow and the Ukraine. Became a member of the Party's Central Committee in 1934, of its Political Bureau in 1939. During World War II, sat on Military Councils of the Kiev Special Military District, Southwestern direction, Stalingrad, Southern and First Ukrainian fronts. Chairman, Ukrainian Council of Ministers, 1947; Secretary of the Central Committee, Communist Party of the Soviet Union, and First Secretary of the Moscow Regional Committee, 1949–53; member of the Presidium, 1952-64. His leadership, following Stalin's, was notable for relaxation of internal restrictions, increased emphasis on production of consumer goods, and a foreign policy of 'peaceful co-existence' and competition with the west.

My photographic journey to the Soviet Union began in Chicago, when a member of a Russian cultural exchange group in my lecture audience asked, 'And why, among all these portraits of great world personalities, is none of my countrymen represented?' To which I replied, 'Because I have not been invited to visit the U.S.S.R.' This was the stimulus to send a copy of my book, *Portraits of Greatness*, directly to Chairman Khrushchev. ~ After some months, the Soviet Ambassador in Ottawa phoned, greatly excited: the Chairman was pleased with my work. 'This is as good,' he exclaimed, 'as an engraved invitation from the White House or Buckingham Palace.' ~ In Moscow, many outstanding personalities in the sciences and arts and letters sat before my camera, but Khrushchev himself was on vacation at the Black Sea. How could I return home without a portrait of the most powerful of all Russians and the members of his Praesidium? The Foreign Office asked me how much time I would require with the Chairman. 'That's a difficult question,' I answered. 'I had half a minute with De Gaulle, forty minutes with Kennedy, an hour and a half with Pope John, and two days each with Sibelius, Casals, and Schweitzer. Take an average.' ~ On April 21, 1963, Moscow's first real spring day, we were driven to Khrushchev's official dacha (country home) outside the capital, a large, impersonal guest house free of ornamentation. The atmosphere was very relaxed. At precisely the appointed hour, twelve noon, Khrushchev and (to my surprise and delight) his entire family strolled across the wide lawn, their faces tanned and smiling. ~ As I watched Khrushchev's portly figure approaching, suddenly I thought, 'Here is a personality I must photograph in a big fur coat.' I asked the Press Officer for such a coat. He shook his head, '*Niet.*' My wife asked Mrs. Khrushchev; alas, the garment was in mothballs in their Moscow apartment. ~ After making formal photographs of the affable Chairman, I switched the lights off, and to the surprise of the interpreter, I asked Khrushchev directly. 'Why not?' he replied, 'Of course.' Soon an aide appeared, weighed down under the most voluminous fur I have ever seen. The Chairman then sent the aide to his private dacha nearby to fetch the knitted woollen stocking cap to complete the costume. 'You must take the picture quickly,' the Chairman smiled, donning the coat, 'or this snow leopard will devour me.' ~ Mrs. Khrushchev, who was chatting with my wife, was astonished when the fur appeared. She bent forward intimately, and, with a twinkle in her eye, recollected, 'You know, that coat is the very one Harold Macmillan wore when he and my husband went tobogganing here together. Mr. Macmillan fell off—but my husband did not!' The Chairman exclaimed, 'This is Canada Day! Not only are you photographing me, but your Ambassador, Arnold Smith, at my invitation, flew today to Siberia to inspect installations. It is the first such tour by any Western diplomat.' ~ I asked Khrushchev whether he felt more at ease with the then-new 'hot line' from Moscow to Washington. 'Yes,' he said, 'but we need more than a hot line to save the world from chaos. We need a meeting of minds.' ~ Of course, I could not foresee then that, within eighteen months, this remarkable personage would be out of office. But on hearing the news of his fall, I could not doubt that in Russian history he would always remain a formidable landmark, the agent or at least the symbol of a decisive and hopeful change in his nation's life. Here, I venture to think, is the face of the eternal peasant, perhaps the collective portrait of a great people, painted like Cromwell, warts and all.

Martin Luther King, Jr.

American clergyman and leader in the civil rights movement. Born 1929 in Atlanta, Georgia. Killed by assassination in Memphis, Tennessee, in April 1968. Educated Morehouse College, Crozer Theological Seminary, Boston University. Pastor, Dexter Avenue Baptist Church, Montgomery, Alabama. President, Montgomery Improvement Association. Founder and leader, Southern Christian Leadership Council. Author of *Stride Towards Freedom*, *Strength to Love*, *Why We Can't Wait*. Received several honorary degrees and other awards. Nobel Peace Prize winner, 1964.

In August 1962 I was asked to hurry down to Atlanta, Georgia, to photograph the Reverend Martin Luther King for a national publication. He had just returned home from nearby Albany, where for months he had been leading the most concentrated and sustained assault on segregation seen till then in the South. Inspired by his oratory and example, hundreds of Negroes of all ages and backgrounds had allowed themselves to be herded into jail until the cells overflowed with their protest. He himself had been vilified, attacked, arrested twice; he, too, had spent time in jail. I found him tired, but harbouring no hatred, not even disapproval. He sought only that he and his people should be treated as first-class citizens. ~ This portrait was taken under the most difficult conditions. We had very little time, and the only place available was a corner of Mr. King's church. Nowhere could he relax when constantly beset by friends and aides wishing him well, commiserating on his difficulties, congratulating him upon his return, planning new strategy. What emerged in my mind and, I trust, in the portrait, was the dedication of the man and his clear vision of ultimate victory. This young minister, only 33 when the picture was taken, had been leading the civil rights battle since the bus boycott in Montgomery six years earlier. He had already seen many barriers fall; he had helped to engender a new spirit. 'Without a movement like the one in Albany,' he said, 'thousands of Negroes would still be walking around with their heads buried. Now they have become organized and articulate. They walk with a new sense of dignity and self-respect.' ~ What of the future? He warned of a potential new militancy. He feared that his people would depart from the non-violent civil disobedience he had learned from Gandhi and always followed. Negroes must act, he said, but not with hatred. 'Only when the people act are the rights on paper given life. But they must never use second-class methods to gain those rights. We must never succumb to the temptation to use violence.' ~ As I flew back to Ottawa that evening and the quiet coolness of Little Wings, my home on the Rideau River, I thought of something else he had said: 'No social advance rolls in on the wheels of inevitability. It comes through the tireless efforts and persistent work of dedicated individuals.' No man in America personified better than Martin Luther King the dedication of his people to their inalienable rights.

Roppeita Kita

Japanese Noh player, born in Tokyo in 1874. The popularity of the Noh plays had begun to decline after the Meiji restoration in 1868; a subsequent revival of interest in the tradition was largely due to his influence. He became the 14th head of the Kitaryu school of Noh players and a member of the Art Academy of Japan.

Roppeita Kita is more than a legend in Japan, he is a living shrine—so revered that all who enter the theatre when he is on stage fall to their knees in respect. At 90-plus, he is one of the greatest actors of the Noh drama, a form of theatre which has been so meticulously refined over seven centuries, so filled with subtle symbolism, that even few contemporary Japanese can fully appreciate all the nuances of the performance. To the Western eye, it is fascinating but totally alien. ~ Kita's son, and his grandson, act in the same Noh company. The graceful young man in the portrait is Kita's grandson; I wanted to include him to stress the continuity of tradition. He proved most helpful, as well, in conveying messages by shouting—with the utmost respect—into the elder's ear. ~ The photograph was taken on the stage of the Kita Noh Theatre in Tokyo. The painted screen in the background is the only scenery: the pine trees are symbolic of the Noh drama—and of eternity. The white post behind Kita serves a more practical purpose. Two such posts on the stage help to orient the principal actor, whose vision is restricted by the narrow eyeholes of an elaborate wooden mask. (The second actor is not permitted to wear the mask; he must make his face as mask-like as possible.) ~ The masks worn in Noh drama represent the nature of the characters portrayed. Before each performance, an actor imbues himself with that spirit, taking the mask reverently from its lacquer box, donning it, and communing with it before the mirror. If he is not in complete possession of the spirit of the mask, he fears, it will show on stage in his hands and gestures, even in his way of breathing. This is more than putting on make-up; it is psychological transformation. ~ There are no women in the Noh theatre; all feminine roles are played by men. Even the strongest, most virile actors are changed, and not only in carriage and movements: they seem to take on a feminine soul and spirit as well. Kita's own favourite role was the Princess, an angel who descends from heaven to dance for a fisherman who has found her robe, in the play, *Hagoromo*. (Perhaps this attraction is connected with his former passion for fishing—a hobby he can no longer pursue, nor, alas, can he now even eat the fish that others catch.) ~ Before we went on the stage, we sat and talked in his dressing room while Kita smoked a cigar. Not until a few years ago was it permitted to illumine the Noh stage with incandescent light, and then only for brief periods. I asked, did he mind photographers, since it is absolutely forbidden to photograph the play itself. The old man admitted that once the idea of a camera portrait, particularly on stage, would have been abhorrent. But right after the war, American soldiers used to give him cigarettes, and in return for such treasures he had felt obliged to let them take his picture. Now he was used to it. His allergy to film had been overcome—through an addiction.

Jacques Lipchitz

Sculptor, born in Lithuania in 1891. At eighteen went to Paris, where he studied sculpture at the École des Beaux Arts and the Académie Julian. First exhibited in 1912 at the Salon d'Automne and the Salon National des Beaux Arts; first one-man show, 1920. Continued working in Paris until just before its occupation by the Germans, when he escaped to the south of France. In 1941 went to the United States, where he became established in New York through a series of one-man shows, and where he has since earned an international reputation as an innovator in sculpture.

The vital patriarch of contemporary sculpture, Jacques Lipchitz—a massive man, no longer ramrod straight, but very strong—studied me intently as I arranged my lighting and camera at his Hastings-on-Hudson, New York, home. 'What a head to sculpt,' he murmured, 'I should like to do you in bronze.' I thought then that this 70-odd-year-old giant was just being polite. But when he telephoned to me three weeks later, and reiterated that 'I really mean it and I *am* serious,' we agreed to meet again in Italy. The tables were turned, and this time it was I who would be the subject! ~ The Fonderia d'Arte of Luigi Tommasi in the Tuscan hamlet of Pietrasanta is where Lipchitz works most of the year. The location is in the tradition of great sculpture. Near the foundry are the Carrara marble quarries, and the path Michelangelo trod during the Renaissance in search of perfect white stone is still used today. The village is a magnet which draws pilgrims from the world of art, letters, and society. ~ Observing Lipchitz' method of working was absorbing. He works in a very pure fashion; one piercing glance and an image begins to form from the inert clay—with such intensity that any interruption shatters his mood. I soon found that if I said anything, just to lighten the creative tension, he would be completely distracted. ~ I sat for him seven mornings, an hour and a half each day with a five-minute break at midpoint. We would then repair for lunch to what he called the 'Labourers' Club.' I discovered this meant *creative* labourers—those who worked in the foundry transforming Lipchitz' small maquettes into colossal bronze reality. ~ The atmosphere of the club was like an idyll from an ancient Roman poet—the simplest of wooden benches, gravel floors, a roof of vines in the open air, good wine. Lipchitz enjoyed the honesty and earthiness of these surroundings. ~ Another aspect of Lipchitz—his extreme sophistication—is evident in his villa, a sixteenth-century structure he and his wife, Yulla, have renovated over the past seven years. Proud African warrior heads and animals stand silhouetted against the landscape from the loggia. ~ There is a magnificent collection of archaic statues and artifacts from man's ancient past. Of these, Lipchitz remarked, 'It's not only the aesthetic aspect (of these artifacts) which interests me, but the men who did it—what they felt. The men...from all the ages...are with me in this collection.' ~ It is his second such collection; the first he lost when he fled penniless from Europe to New York in 1941. After 1945 he scoured the Continent seeking his lost treasures, almost, as he put it, 'like a centipede looking frantically for a lost arm.' Now, he told us, he would never repeat this desperate search: 'I have finally learned to live every day and not regret the past.' ~ One of the fascinating evenings of my life was spent on the Lipchitz loggia. Gathered together were three titans of contemporary sculpture: Lipchitz himself, Marino Marini, and Henry Moore. There was no common language in which all were fluent. Conversation was a polyglot of English, French, and Italian, yet there was great understanding between them. ~ Beyond them stretched miles of Tuscan landscape that resembled a Renaissance painting. As I watched, the scene was pierced by storms and lightning, then cleared, then storms returned. It was a thrilling, almost Wagnerian, reminder, in the presence of great art, of the spectacular power of nature.

Giacomo Manzù

Italian sculptor, born in Bergamo in 1908. At eleven became apprentice to a craftsman who specialized in church decorations; later attended evening classes in plastic arts. First one-man show of sculpture, Rome, 1938. First came to international attention when awarded the Grand Prix in Italian Sculpture at the Venice Biennale in 1948. Work has been exhibited in major museums in the United States and Europe. Until 1954 was Professor of Sculpture at the Academy of Fine Arts of Brera in Milan. Among his major works are the main doors of Salzburg Cathedral, the *Porta delle Morte* in St. Peter's in Rome, and the *Porta della Pace e della Guerra* of St. Laurenz Church, Rotterdam. Awarded the Lenin Peace Prize in 1966. *The Artist and the Pope* by Curtis Bill Pepper (Giniger, 1968) described the development of his friendship with Pope John XXIII, who had invited his fellow townsman to sculpt his portrait.

It is many kilometers from Rome to Giacomo Manzù's almost baronial holdings in the town of Ardea. Not only did we travel there for photography, but we were on an informal errand. Our mutual friend, the famous Italian men's designer, Angelo Litrico, had just completed a brocade evening jacket for the sculptor, and we were delivering it personally. ~ As we drove up to the main house, we noticed a stooped and massive man entering one the outbuildings, walking with such singular concentration that we were reminded of a bull making his way, oblivious of anything else. We realized later that this determined figure had been Manzù. ~ One of the first things we saw upon entering his main hall was a huge rack of hats, one for every conceivable occasion, all perched at rakish angles—next to an exquisite Greek torso. There we were met by our host's young wife, Inge, a ballerina who had modelled for him in Munich and is still the frequent inspiration for much of his work. She hung the elaborate evening jacket between the hats and the Greek torso, creating still another study in contrasts, and we were led into the huge living room. ~ Manzù entered, pervading the formal salon with his enormous peasant vigour, wearing a hat with a feather. He did not remove that hat all afternoon. ~ Manzù makes no bones about the fact that he was born a peasant, in Bergamo, where Pope John XXIII also grew up. As a successful artist, he has fulfilled the dream of every peasant, to own much land, to drink much wine, to enjoy much luxury. He drove us to his studio, a large barn near the house. No one walks in his menage; they drive, even if the distance is only fifty or sixty yards. ~ In the barn, and in smaller neighbouring sheds, stood a small army of cardinals in plaster and other media in various stages of completion. Manzù's fascination with cardinals as a subject stems from his early youth when, in his native medieval hill town, the processions of prelates, in their gorgeous pyramidal robes moving with stately grace, almost like chess pieces propelled from beneath, etched themselves on his inner eye. ~ We discussed whether we might take some photographs of him at a nearby museum of his sculpture, Amici Manzù (The Friends of Manzù). He adamantly refused; if he were going to be photographed, it was to be on his own soil. ~ During our photographic session, he spoke tenderly of his great friendship with Pope John XXIII. Although Manzù was a professed Communist, and his work was condemned by the Holy Office during the Ministry of Pius XII, Pope John XXIII had invited his fellow townsman to sculpt his portrait and, ultimately, his death mask. Manzù told us many of the experiences that appear in Curtis Bill Pepper's fascinating account, *The Artist and the Pope*. When Manzù confessed to the Pope he was confused because, after two fruitless attempts, he could not yet find the inner core of His Holiness, the Pope responded, 'Yes, but there are confusions in any search. What matters is that you seek. Also that you love humanity. Otherwise, you wouldn't spend a lifetime creating it with your hands and your heart.' ~ The late July afternoon grew hotter and hotter, but we were both oblivious of the extreme heat. Together we enjoyed a bottle of champagne Manzù opened to celebrate the photography. Manzù maintained the peasant mask with much knee-slapping, Italian jokes, and earthy expressions. But, as he briefly touched one of his cardinals, his inner artistic reverence revealed itself. ~ As we were packing the equipment, Inge sent over a pot of tea on exquisite china, and she and Manzù left. Only later did we learn that they had had an appointment for two hours earlier, at a town 30 miles away. Such was Manzù's consideration and respect, he had not thought of cutting our time short.

Marcel Marceau

French mime, creator of the character, 'Bip.' Born in Strasbourg, 1923; studied at the Ecole des Beaux-Arts in Paris and was a pupil of the famous actor and teacher Charles Dullin; soon after he created his own company, the Compagnie de Mime Marcel Marceau. Appeared at Paris theatres where his success led him to undertake a tour overseas; has now been seen on several tours in the United States and Canada.

From the start everything went badly in my attempt to photograph Marcel Marceau, the great French mime. I had arranged a sitting in Montreal, in 1956, where I would stop on my way to the United States, but at the appointed hour I found that all my equipment had been shipped, by mistake, straight through to New York. However, some weeks later, M. Marceau arrived in New York for further stage appearances and a new appointment was set in my studio-apartment. I felt, after the Montreal fiasco, that I owed my subject unusual politeness but, in my efforts to please him, let the situation get entirely out of hand. ~ The actor had his own preconceived ideas about the portrait he wanted. In fact, as I was about to conclude the sitting I suddenly realized that I had been recording all those familiar poses, attitudes, and expressions that I had seen on the stage. To avoid doing this I had already asked him not to use his white-face make-up, so that I could see the abounding mobility of his own face. Thus, in the concluding moments, I was compelled to be quite firm with him. Though he may have doubted their wisdom, he took my suggestions well. ~ M. Marceau has very definite theories of art and some particular preferences. He is particularly enamoured of his portrayal of 'Death' in his famous sketch, 'Youth, Maturity, Old Age, and Death,' and feels that at the end of this sequence he really dies and leaves this world! I think he almost believes it as a fact. ~ In the course of a long, random conversation, he told me an amusing story about his son Michel, then seven years old. He had become his father's most ardent admirer and at the conclusion of every performance led the applause with shouts of 'Bravo, Papa, bravo!' M. Marceau warned the boy repeatedly that this sort of thing was not done, yet invariably, as the curtain descended, the father heard the son's small familiar voice. He told me that it was highly embarrassing, but I could see that he loved it. ~ The actor may fancy his role as 'Death,' but my favourite in his diverse repertoire is 'The Butterfly.' In it he seems 90 per cent butterfly, 10 per cent human being (or is it *vice versa*?) and I always think of him thus, flitting through life with a butterfly's delight plainly visible on that ever changing sensitive face.

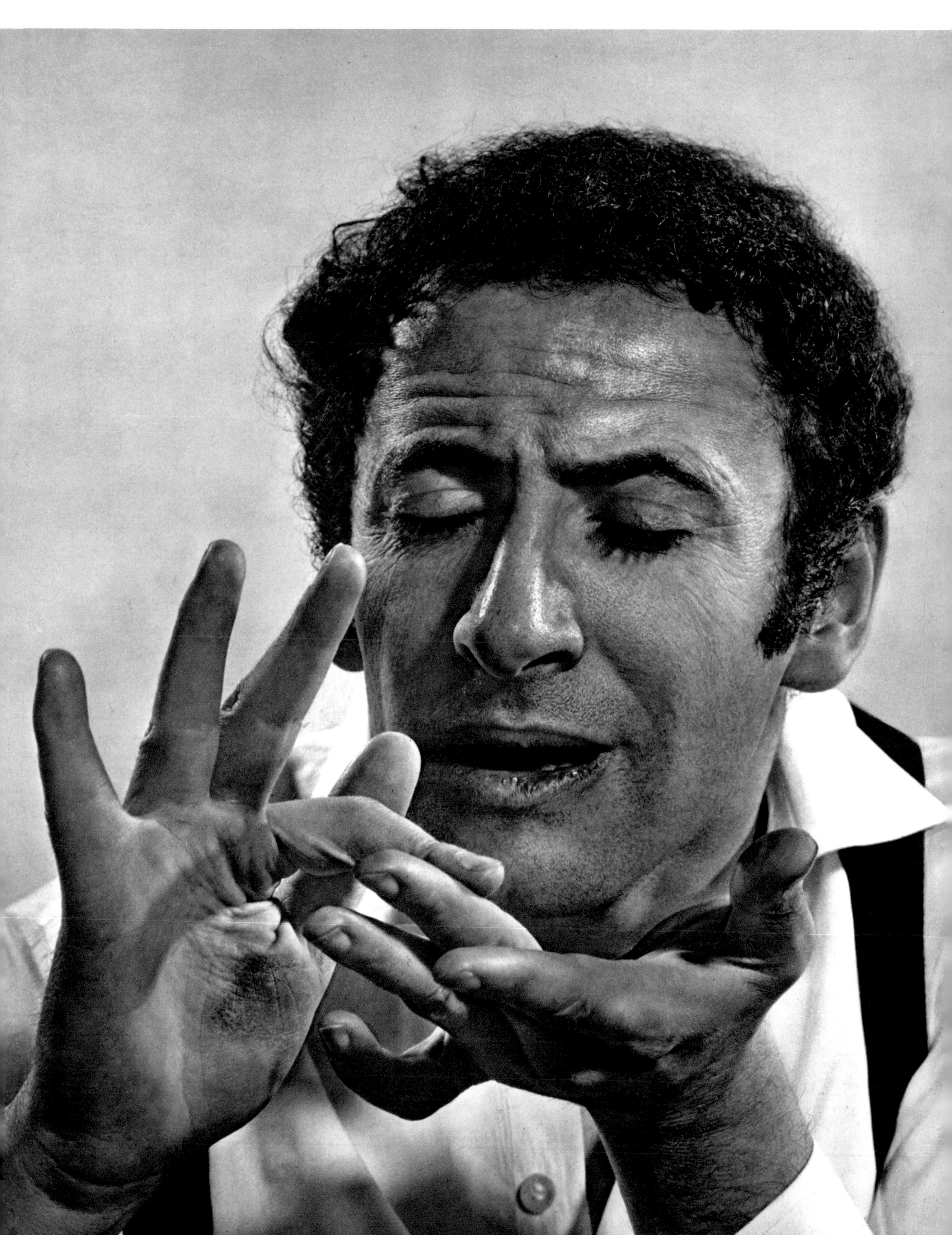

Marino Marini

Italian sculptor. Born 1901. Titular Professor of Sculpture at the Academy of Fine Arts of Brera in Milan since 1940. Educated at the Academy of Fine Arts in Florence. Professor at the Scuola d'Arte de Villa Reale in Monza, 1929–40. His works have been exhibited extensively in North America and in Europe, and he has received many international awards and honours.

The Etruscan-spirited horses and riders for which this great Italian sculptor is best known have always spoken to me of a joyful, untrammelled childhood of liberation and hope. When I met Marino Marini in Tuscany, at Jacques Lipchitz' villa, he was all I had anticipated—completely sincere, open of mind and heart, without any side. He speaks simply. His country home, which I expected to be full of memorabilia, was almost austere in decor. ~ We dined together two or three times while I was in Tuscany in 1969. The more I saw of him and his wife, the more I loved them. She is a wonderfully vivacious companion who, with him, forms a perfect unit. On my next Italian journey, in 1970, I went prepared to photograph him. ~ On the summer day of that visit, Marini's publisher had just delivered the advance copy of a new deluxe publication of his collected works. He invited my wife and me to examine the reproductions. Signora Marini translated our responses. To my surprise, as we turned the pages, our attention was riveted not only on the horses and riders, but on the sculptor's lesser-known portrait busts, which were beautifully photographed. Marini does not strike one as being harsh or judgmental, yet these heads revealed an inner eye that was relentlessly honest and thought-provoking—not mean, but absolutely true in recognizing hitherto unplumbed dimensions in the character of the sitter. ~ Estrellita, my wife, began describing the inner character of the Marini portraits she saw in the book. Then the Marinis would tell us (if we had not known) who the person was. In some portraits, the traits Estrellita detected were not altogether complimentary, and the Marinis smiled conspiratorially at one another in silent and somewhat rueful agreement. But, at one page, Estrellita exclaimed, 'Ah, this is a medieval princess who is sincere, without guile, beautiful, and so very feminine. I like her!' Our companions went into gales of laughter. It was a head of Mrs. Marini executed some years ago. I smiled at the Marinis—silently heaving a sigh of relief. ~ Marini's portraits are invariably smaller than life. The one he is holding in the photograph is of the composer, Igor Stravinsky. It was the only piece of three-dimensional art in his house at the time. The sculptor's aristocratic face reveals his fundamental compassion, but no less the absolute sureness and integrity of his vision.

William Somerset Maugham
C.H.

British novelist and dramatist (1874–1965). Educated at King's School, Canterbury; Heidelberg University; and St. Thomas's Hospital, where he studied medicine. His novels include: *Liza of Lambeth, Of Human Bondage, The Moon and Sixpence, The Painted Veil, Cakes and Ale, The Razor's Edge*. He wrote also many plays, some of which have become classics of the modern theatre: *The Circle, The Letter, The Constant Wife*. His brilliant short stories remain very popular and have been the basis of several films.

The face of Somerset Maugham—a deeply lined, wise, and almost ageless face—is as familiar to the world as are the writer's teeming works. Yet the man I discovered in the grand suite of a New York hotel in 1950 entirely surprised me. He was quite unlike the man I had expected from reading his stories and many articles about him. ~ Apparently he had kept his appointment with me by interrupting his customary afternoon nap. The black eye-shield he wore at such times still dangled from his hand. Though he obviously would have preferred to rest (for he was by then an 'old party' as he always told reporters), he gave me his whole attention and almost charmed me away from the business of the sitting. ~ To begin with, his face was arresting—not handsome, of course, in any conventional sense but impressive, rather like the carved, wooden image of some tribal god in the South Seas where he roamed so often. The eyes were penetrating, almost hypnotic and intensely alive. That well-known expression of starkness (often taken for cynicism) broke frequently into the most engaging smile. To my surprise Maugham, the realist, the hard-boiled sceptic, possessed an irresistible warmth. This made the work of the camera easy but did not help my other purpose. I wanted to ask him a thousand questions about his methods, his life, and his views, but after half an hour I realized that I, not he, was being interviewed. Out of long habit, I suppose, he automatically began to draw a stranger out. His curiosity about human nature was insatiable in his old age. He found in everybody, even the chance passer-by, the possibility of some quirk or anecdote that had in it the making of a tale after passing through the alchemy of his imagination. I had the sudden vivid feeling that he viewed the human comedy with the objectivity of my camera. ~ At any rate, Mr. Maugham talked little and I am afraid that I talked much, simply because I could not resist a man who appeared to have no interest in the world just then but me. Doubtless that was his custom with everyone who crossed his path; the result is known to just about everyone who reads his stories. ~ Mr. Maugham was not in a talking mood that day, but I have heard that in this respect his mood could change. A close friend of his remarked to me, later, that Maugham 'when he gets going is an extraordinarily interesting talker and talks as well as he writes. Yes, and he reads his stories aloud as well as any actor could.' ~ I remember Somerset Maugham, then, rather as a polished, elegant, and sympathetic listener, with an immense cunning in penetrating another man's innermost thoughts.

François Mauriac

French poet, playwright, and novelist (1885–1970). Was brought up in strict Roman Catholic orthodoxy by his widowed mother, educated at Bordeaux University and the Ecole des Chartes in Paris. His first literary success was *Le Baiser au lépreux*, published in 1922. Other works include *Génitrix*, *Le Nœud de vipères*, *Asmodée* (a play), and *Le Sagouin*. During World War II he worked for the French Resistance and wrote a 'Cahier noir' for the clandestinely published *Editions de minuit*. After the war he contributed to *Figaro*, *Figaro littéraire*, and *La Table ronde*. Won the Grand Prix of the Académie Française, 1926, and the Nobel Prize for Literature, 1952.

It is quite absurd—I speak with strong conviction and somewhat bitter experience—to say that the French are a decadent race. How can they be when so many of them climb six flights of stairs several times a day? Indeed, most of the great Frenchmen I have photographed have chosen to live on the sixth floor, or higher, without an elevator—François Mauriac, the eminent and devout Catholic writer, for example. Such stamina and asceticism would be unthinkable in the vigorous New World. ~ Since M. Mauriac could not be asked to come down from his Olympian heights, I and my assistant were compelled to ascend, with all our heavy photographic equipment, in several breath-taking climbs. And then, after all the wires had been connected, there was no electricity! So we waited hopefully, on that day in 1949, for the Paris power to be turned on again. ~ Since he lived by choice under such difficult conditions, I was not entirely surprised to find M. Mauriac sunk in profound pessimism. Apparently he saw nothing to encourage him in the state of the world and was entirely convinced that civilization must ultimately face a third, devastating war. He spoke in a strange, muffled voice, which he explained as the result of an operation. ~ While we waited for electricity, he talked freely on many subjects of a philosophical sort. I deliberately needled him a bit on his familiar journalistic feud with Sartre and the existentialists, then the prevailing fad in France. M. Mauriac was most definitely anti-Sartre, whom he considered an apostle of negation, a very bad and dangerous state of mind to be nourished among the French people. Evidently M. Mauriac had done his best to discourage this movement and, with an air of triumph, he showed me a newspaper article in which, it appeared, he had entirely vanquished Sartre. ~ We had been talking for a long time but still there was no electricity and I was on the point of despair. Yet after climbing those endless stairs with all my photographic paraphernalia I did not intend to leave empty-handed and undergo the same ordeal a second time. ~ On the off chance of success, I placed my subject before an open French door and against the greyest of Parisian skies. My assistant removed a sheet from the bed and held it up as a reflector. The resulting profile portrait, I feel, conveys François Mauriac's Gallic charm and perhaps something of his dark despondency about human affairs.

Marshall McLuhan
C.C.

Canadian author, university professor, and communications specialist. Born 1911. Educated at University of Manitoba and Cambridge University, and has taught at universities in the United States and Canada since 1936. Professor of English, University of Toronto since 1946 and now Director of its Centre for Culture and Technology. Schweitzer Professor in the Humanities at Fordham University, 1967–8. His many publications have given rise to considerable controversy, as has his theory that civilization is being reshaped by the nature of the media used for communication rather than by their content ('the medium is the message'). Has received numerous international literary awards and honours.

No collection of faces of our time would be complete without the guru of the electronic age, the most talked about academic figure in North America. Marshall McLuhan's name became, in the 1960s, if not a household word, certainly a cocktail party cliché, even spawning a popular adjective, 'McLuhanesque,' to describe similarities to his theories or, alternatively, his manner of expression. ~ His analysis of the changes in society that have come with the advance of the electronic media, both 'cool' and 'hot,' are based on evident brilliance and broad scholarship; yet they are at times couched in such cryptic, oracular, even outrageous fashion as to make them as difficult to accept as they may be to understand. Still they are taken almost as gospel by many. Successful advertising campaigns, including even one for the presidency of the United States, have been based on their message. ~ We had arranged to meet in his book-filled office in one corner of the University of Toronto campus, where he has been professor of English for many years. For hours he talked almost continuously, interestingly, quotably: it was absolutely fascinating, but at the end of it I was exhausted, and suggested we wait for photography until the next day. Yet engaging as are his mind and personality, I can remember little of what he said then. We have since had other good long walks and talks together, at Toronto and at Fordham University where he held the Albert Schweitzer chair for a year. Nevertheless, I must admit regretfully that the more I have found myself with him, the less I have retained from his philosophy. ~ At our second meeting, I announced: 'Photography first, then talk.' We had arranged to have the sitting in a gallery of the Royal Ontario Museum, designed by one of his colleagues to display the early development of life in prehistoric seas. Many novel ideas had been employed to involve the visitor, including tape-recorded explanations transmitted by telephone. The background was intriguing. It seemed to reflect McLuhan's interests in broad reaches of time and in the electronic extensions man has developed to the human nervous system. ~ Some time later, I had an opportunity to introduce McLuhan to two of the most important advertising executives in the Americas. The four of us spent an extremely agreeable and stimulating evening together. At the end of it one of the executives thought McLuhan was a genius; the other emphatically did not—which seems to sum up the general division of opinion—and the influence of the man.

Joan Miró

Spanish surrealist artist. Born in 1893; studied art in Barcelona; went to Paris in 1919 and in the twenties joined the surrealist movement. His work is distinguished by the use of pure colours, delicate lines, and abstract shapes. Although best known as a painter, he has also worked in ceramics, sculpture, engraving, and lithography. In 1959 he was awarded the Guggenheim Prize for two ceramic murals for the Unesco Building in Paris. Now divides his time between Paris and Palma de Majorca. (A print of this portrait has been acquired by the Philadelphia Museum of Art.)

The self-effacement of this great Spanish painter is well known to anyone who has interviewed him. He is pleasant; he co-operates; but he gives little of himself away and is rarely photographed. Yet his portrait was one that I was most anxious to add to a special exhibition of 'Men Who Make Our World' which I was assembling for EXPO, the 1967 World's Fair in Montreal. All this was in my mind as we approached Studio Maeght in the suburbs of Paris where Joan Miró was completing a new set of lithographs. ~ Inside, the building looked like any small printing plant—a prosaic setting for a master of fantasy and symbolism. In one room a man sat working. He was a type that could blend with any wallpaper. His clothes were extraordinary: silks, velvets, suedes, a combination of the Côte d'Azur and Capri. But on him they looked like overalls, three hues darker than life. So pervasive was Miró's personal reticence that it overwhelmed even the opulence of his costume. ~ He has written, 'A man's life, as others know it, is not the real one, but only a semblance they construct. The real Miró is as truly what I am to myself as what others—and perhaps even I—conceive of me as being. Isn't the essential self to be found in that mysterious area where creation takes place...?' How was I to separate the clothes from the man? How to capture the essential self? ~ I set to work. Miró was agreeable. Gradually he began to realize that portraiture, as well as painting, might be an art; and slowly but perceptibly the layers around him peeled off. Once or twice he looked up, and for a moment a twinkle came into his eyes. I placed one of his unfinished lithographs before him: he studied it, and became lost in communion with the works of his imagination. ~ At last I asked, 'Do you usually look like that when you work?' With a deprecating little smile, he took off the beautiful suede jacket he had worn for the portrait, and put on a well-worn, paint-stained sweater. Now he began to relax, still contemplating his work. ~ Then I said, 'It's rather chilly. Don't you wear a hat?' Almost apologetically, but very happily, as if he were relieved to stop posing, he went over to a closet and pulled out a battered and mellow old hat. He sat down again, put it on, and looked up as if to say, 'So, you found me out.' ~ At that moment of revelation I released the shutter. The camera, I hope, has found him out.

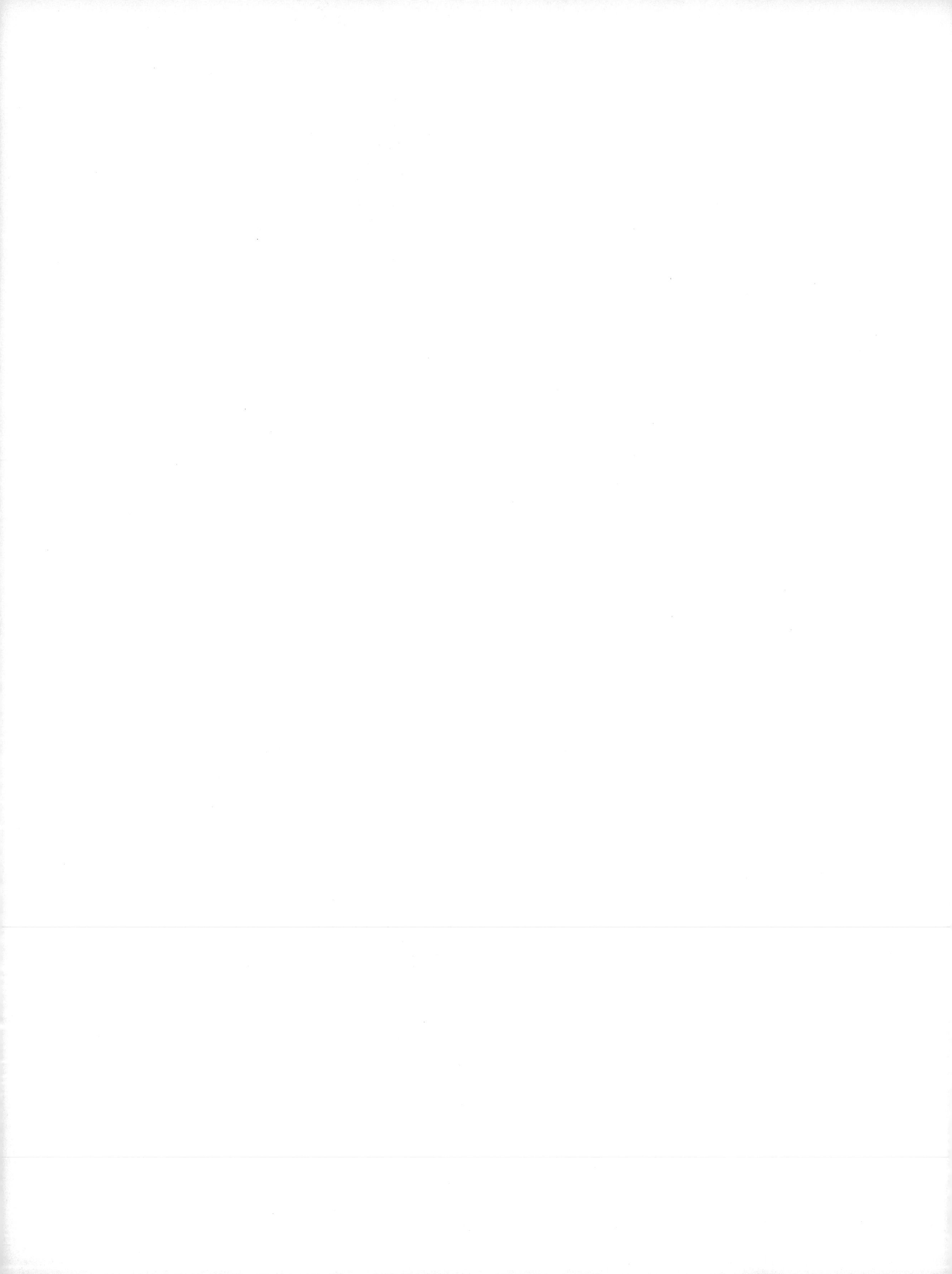

Richard M. Nixon

37th President of the United States. Born in 1913 in Yorba Linda, California. Educated at Whittier College and Duke University Law School. After practising law in Whittier, became an attorney with the Office of Emergency Management in Washington. From 1942 to 1946 served in the U.S. Navy, ending his service as a Lieutenant-Commander. Member of Congress for the 12th California District, 1947–51; U.S. Senator from California, 1951–3; Vice-President of the United States under President Eisenhower, 1953–61 (second youngest vice-president in the history of the United States). Ran unsuccessfully for the presidency in 1960 against John F. Kennedy, and as Republican candidate for the governorship of California in 1962. Returned to legal practice until his election as President in 1968.

When this picture was taken, Richard Nixon was just a week away from the dream that had shaped his 56 years. He was about to be sworn in as the 37th President of the United States. ~ He was the poor boy who had reached his nation's highest office, the loser who had bounced back from political wilderness to stubbornly fashion victory, the often lonely, private individual who had been elected by the great mass of Middle America. In 1960, after his first attempt for the presidency, he had remarked that 'defeat is a greater test of character than victory.' Now he was prepared to admit that 'winning is a lot more fun.' ~ I had been asked to take his portrait by *Newsweek* magazine. Mrs. Nixon was the first to arrive at the hotel suite that had been set up as a temporary studio. We chatted easily for a while, trying to think of names for a new puppy the Nixons had been given, discussing some of the great problems of poverty, war, and unrest that her husband would have to deal with. Then the President-elect arrived. ~ He was wearing a blue suit and tie, was tanned, and almost electrifyingly jovial. We recalled a previous photographic session which had produced a portrait he had distributed to colleagues across the country. Then, 'Tell me something about your swinging new Canadian Prime Minister,' he asked. I obliged with some of the better known anecdotes about Mr. Trudeau. The atmosphere of the session was very light and humorous. But pressure was great, and in less than half an hour the Nixons were forced to leave. ~ Presumably what was most on his mind at that period was the Inauguration Speech he would shortly be giving in Washington, in which he called on all Americans to go forward together: 'We today can build a great cathedral of the spirit—each of us raising it one stone at a time, as he reaches out to his neighbour, helping, caring, doing.'

Georgia O'Keeffe

American artist. Born 1887 in Sun Prairie, Wisconsin. Studied at Art Institute of Chicago (1904–5), Art Students' League, New York (1907–8), University of Virginia (1912), and Columbia University (1914–16). Commercial artist, 1909; supervisor of art for the public schools of Amarillo, Texas, 1912–14; instructor in art, University of Virginia, summers, 1913–16; head of art department, West Texas State Normal College, Canyon, Texas, 1916–18. Has confined activities to painting since 1918. Became one of a group (including Marin and Dove) sponsored by the photographer Alfred Stieglitz, whom she married in 1924. Paintings first exhibited by him at 291 Fifth Avenue, and later at the Intimate Gallery and An American Place. After her husband's death in 1946 she spent three years cataloguing his collection and distributing it to major centres in the United States. Since 1949 has lived in New Mexico. Best known as a highly original and daring flower painter, she is represented in the Tate Gallery, London, the Metropolitan Museum of Art, New York (which has also purchased a print of this photographic portrait), and the museums of Brooklyn, Cleveland, Detroit, Springfield, Mass., and Washington, D.C.

'At last, a woman on paper.' These were the words uttered by Alfred Stieglitz when he first saw the drawings of the artist Georgia O'Keeffe, whom he was later to marry. When I came to Abiquiu, New Mexico, in 1956 to photograph this remarkable woman who has so enriched American art, I expected to find some of the poetic intensity of her paintings reflected in her personality. Intensity I found, but it was the austere intensity of dedication to her work which has led Miss O'Keeffe to cut out of her life anything that might interfere with her ability to express herself in paint. Her friend and fellow artist Anita Pollitzer has commented perceptively on Miss O'Keeffe: 'A solitary person, with terrific powers of concentration, she is so in love with the thing she does that she subordinates all else in order to win time and freedom to paint. . . . She has worked out a simple, well-considered pattern of life, so unvaried that the average person would refuse to live it, and she refuses to allow anything to pull her away from it. People figure very slightly in her world. . . . Her decisions as to her use of time are very definite. Last year [1949] she said to me: "I know I am unreasonable about people but there are so many wonderful people whom I *can't take the time* to know." She says that even in her student days she saw that dancing at night meant daytime lost from painting—so she refused to dance although she loved it. She decides carefully on each point, what to have and what to give up. There is nothing weak about her willpower. I have never known her to have any regrets or envy.' ~ As though to concentrate her vision inwardly Miss O'Keeffe has banished colour from her surroundings. Her adobe home, with wide windows on every side overlooking the mountains, and almost completely empty of ornament, seemed stark to me, but when I asked Miss O'Keeffe why she chose to live in such a remote area she replied, 'What other place is there?' In the end I decided to photograph her as yet another friend had described her: 'Georgia, her pure profile against the dark wood of the paneling, calm, clear; her sleek black hair drawn swiftly back into a tight knot at the nape of her neck; the strong white hands, touching and lifting everything, even the boiled eggs, as if they were living things—sensitive, slow-moving hands, coming out of the black and white, always this black and white.'

Sir Laurence Olivier

KT.

British actor-manager. Born 1907. First appeared in Shakespearean play at Stratford-on-Avon in 1922; since 1929 has appeared in London, New York, Paris, and other cities in Shakespearean and other roles; co-director, Old Vic Theatre Company, 1944-5, toured with this Company in Australia and New Zealand, 1948. Actor-manager at St. James's Theatre, London, 1950–1, Shakespeare Memorial Theatre, Stratford-on-Avon, 1955; Director, Chichester Festival Theatre, 1962–5; Director, The National Theatre, 1962– . Has played in many films, including *Wuthering Heights, Rebecca, Pride and Prejudice, The Entertainer, Othello;* produced, directed, and starred in film versions of *Henry V, Hamlet,* and *Richard III.* Played several times opposite Vivien Leigh, his former wife. Now married to British actress Joan Plowright. Created Life Peer in 1970, the first actor in British history to be honoured in this way.

When Sir Laurence Olivier greeted me at his London home in 1954, he appeared fatigued. Small wonder, since he had been directing and himself acting in his film production of *Richard III* all day long. Besides, he said, he had been wearing a false nose and various other uncomfortable disguises which converted a handsome contemporary Englishman into the hunchback villain of feudal times. ~ Sir Laurence, and his *petite* wife, Vivien Leigh, made a charming couple and did not grudge me their time even though they were packing for their departure next day to California. ~ Soon after the sitting began, their Siamese cat named Boy leapt upon Sir Laurence's head and completely obscured his face . . . obviously a privileged character of the household. I snapped a few candid pictures of this frivolity to remind me, later on, of a great actor mastered by a pet which alone could steal a scene from him. ~ Presently, while I waited for the right moment for my portrait, Sir Laurence began to talk about the photography used in *Hamlet*. The magnificent depth of field in this film, the sense of grandeur, of distance and mystery were due, he said, to the use of a special lens and to highly imaginative lighting. (He did not mention, of course, the depth, grandeur, and mystery of his direction and acting.) A play like *Hamlet*, he added, was much better filmed in black and white than in colour, for colour would undermine the atmosphere of high tragedy. ~ Several years later, I had an opportunity to meet Sir Laurence again, when he was performing in John Osborne's play *The Entertainer* on Broadway. I had wondered why so great an artist had agreed to act a rather sordid part, created by one of England's 'angry young men.' Sir Laurence saw the play in another light. He said he greatly admired Mr. Osborne's work; in fact, it had been written especially for him, at his own request. ~ I asked him if he felt that the angry young men were significantly affecting the English drama. 'Undoubtedly,' he said. 'But the term "angry young men" is a feeble press epithet and a misnomer. Some of the critics are greatly distorting the fine work of these playwrights. I think they are definitely contributing something to the stage, in form, in content, and in action.' ~ When I asked him what difference he found in British and American audiences he gave me a quick reply: 'I could think of much, much more pleasurable ways of finishing my career than by answering that one!' What, I said, did the movies offer to the serious artist? 'From experience among my friends I would say that financially it is fairly all right in both fields and the choice would be entirely one's own inclination. For myself I enjoy both the theatre and the film media equally but I should say as a general rule that the film is the director's medium and the theatre the actor's medium.'

Robert Oppenheimer

American physicist (1904–1967). Educated at Harvard, Cambridge, and Göttingen. Professor of Physics, University of California and California Institute of Technology, 1929–47; Director, Los Alamos Laboratory, New Mexico, 1943–5; Chairman, General Advisory Committee to the Atomic Energy Commission, 1946–52; Director, Institute for Advanced Study, Princeton, 1947–66. Received the Fermi Award of the U.S. Atomic Energy Commission in 1963.

Dr. Oppenheimer greeted me warmly, in 1956, at the Institute for Advanced Study, Princeton. He remembered that we had met briefly before and now he had left an important conference to keep our appointment. But I detected in this famous scientist a certain brittleness and I thought that the record of deep suffering was written plainly on his face. After his experiences, this was hardly surprising. ~ However, he proved most cooperative and, at my request, wrote down the names of six scientists whom he considered the world's most outstanding. Then, after he had finished, he smiled and added, 'If you asked me for a list tomorrow, most likely I'd give you a different one. Anyway, some of the greatest men of our calling have died recently.' He particularly regretted the untimely passing of Enrico Fermi. ~ But the atmosphere of that sitting was not all sombre. For I had noticed with fascination an oddly shaped pork-pie hat hanging on a peg, the last sort of hat you would expect to see on the head of a sober scientist. The story of that hat tells us something of the other Oppenheimer. He had been presented, he told me, with one of those huge ten-gallon cowboy hats from Texas and, thinking the brim far too wide, had cut it down with a pair of scissors. The result could hardly be called a sartorial triumph. I was happy to see, however, that this scientist, harassed by personal difficulties and by his knowledge of mankind's peril from the discoveries of science, could make a joke of his own. Indeed, I asked him to wear this whimsical headpiece. He did so with a laugh and I photographed him thus to record the thinker's lighter side. ~ But I was aware, of course, that the world of Oppenheimer, behind the genial smile and schoolboy joke, was something like a hundred light years away from my world, or that of any layman. One has only to read some of his simpler speeches and essays to see that this man was probing not only for a knowledge of scientific phenomena useful in our daily life but for ultimate truths explaining the mystery of all life. I could appreciate, however, his blunt dictum on the future of man's life if human intelligence did not catch up with the march of weapons. 'Far beyond disarmament,' he said, 'one has to envisage a world of affirmative collaboration in the world's work between people irrespective of nationality ... the world has to be an open world in which, practically speaking, secrets are illegal.' ~ To such a world Dr. Oppenheimer made, not without great sacrifice, his own unique contribution.

His Holiness Pope Paul VI

263rd Supreme Pontiff of the Roman Catholic Church, elected to the Papacy in June 1963 on the death of Pope John XXIII. Giovanni Battista Montini was born in 1897 in the northern Italian village of Concesio, the son of a politically liberal lawyer-journalist. Educated in nearby Brescia, at Milan, the Gregorian Institute, and the University of Rome. Ordained at Brescia in 1920. Attaché to the Apostolic Nunciature, Warsaw, 1923–24, followed by service in the Vatican Secretariat of State. National Spiritual Director of the Italian Federation of Catholic University Students, 1924–33. Substitute Secretary of State to Cardinal Pacelli (later Pius XII) 1937–39; to Pius XII, 1939–52; Pro-Secretary of State, 1952–54. He was named Archbishop of Milan in 1954 and four years later was made a Cardinal.

I first had the pleasure of photographing Cardinal Montini, as he then was, during the Ecumenical Council. One of the principal figures in its deliberations, he was much pressed for time and could spare only five minutes for the camera. They flew past. Nevertheless, at the end he found additional moments to ask about Canada and my travels, and to give me a small medallion. Probably neither of us suspected that within eight months I would be taking his portrait again as Pontiff. ~ This time I was allowed thirty minutes with him, a generous allocation when he was so busy picking up the many threads of his new office. His Holiness had agreed to appear very informally, wearing only his white cassock and skull-cap. We arranged the lights the night before in one of the three throne rooms. The surroundings—all red brocade and gilt furniture—were ill-suited to a figure so austere and ascetic. Hastily, we set up instead a plain background. ~ Quite early the next morning the Pope entered with his entourage. He walks decisively, with an air of quiet command. I knelt to kiss his ring and receive his blessing. He helped me to rise and we began to work. At the end of half an hour, anxious to gain a little more time, I mentioned to His Holiness that during a recent visit to Moscow I had met Anastas Mikoyan, and had been greeted warmly by him as a fellow Armenian. Mikoyan had said, 'I am glad to meet a countryman who has reached the top of the ladder.' To which I had replied, 'You're very gracious, but you haven't done too badly yourself,' for at the time he was first deputy premier of the Soviet Union. Then I had quickly added, 'We have another Armenian who almost became Pope, Cardinal Agaganian.' Mikoyan replied, 'Yes, we were at the same seminary, but he continued on the wrong track: I do not believe in God.' My little anecdote prompted further conversation with His Holiness and the opportunity to take a few more pictures. ~ He was the third Pope in succession I have had the privilege of photographing. Already he looked as if he had been Pope all his life. Like everyone, I was struck by his ability to combine the strengths of his immediate predecessors. In his gestures, his build, and his austerity, he was reminiscent of Pius XII, to whom he had been very nearly a son. At the same time he showed some of the warmth and openness of John XXIII, to whom he had been so close a friend. ~ He was less easy to know than John, but I sensed that his mind was fixed on the immense details of his office. It was not by choice, I felt, that he seemed remote. Later on, when he had fully mastered his duties, the remoteness would fade and the human being would become clearer in the eye of the world.

The Rt. Hon. Lester B. Pearson
P.C., C.C., O.B.E.

Canadian statesman, Prime Minister of Canada, 1963–8; Leader of the Liberal party, 1958–68. Born 1897; educated at the University of Toronto and St. John's College, Oxford. On teaching staff of the University of Toronto before joining Canadian Department of External Affairs in 1928; Ambassador to the United States, 1945; Secretary of State for External Affairs, 1948–57; Leader of the Opposition, 1958–63. Canadian representative to UNRRA meetings, 1944–6; and Canadian representative at subsequent meetings of the U.N. General Assembly; Chairman, U.N. Political and Security Committee during Special Session of the General Assembly, 1947, and again at 4th Session, 1949; President, 7th Session of the General Assembly, 1952; Canadian representative signing North Atlantic Treaty, 1949; Chairman, North Atlantic Council, 1951–2; Chancellor, Victoria University in the University of Toronto, 1951–8; Chairman, Committee on International Development, 1969; Chancellor, Carleton University, Ottawa since 1969; B.B.C. Reith Lecturer, 1968; Hon. Fellow, St. John's College, Oxford; honorary degrees from 49 universities; Nobel Peace Prize, 1957; Family of Man Award, 1965; Companion of the Order of Canada, 1968.

Quite apart from his political career and even if he had never held elected office, Mr. Pearson would qualify, I think, for any list of the world's leading thinkers. Moreover, the man whom all Canadians and most foreigners know as 'Mike,' is an artist in his way, an artist of humanity, whose canvas is our battered civilization, whose long-sought composition is peace. With his political activities, in a partisan sense, I am not here concerned. He has always fascinated me by his activities in other fields, especially the non-partisan conduct of foreign affairs ... at long and at short range, as a public man, and as a fellow townsman of Ottawa. ~ When I first met and photographed Mr. Pearson, in 1944, he was Canada's Minister to Washington. 'You make me,' he wrote, 'look almost like a statesman.' In fact, my various portraits make him look, I hope, only like the always boyish and sometimes tortured human being that he is. The second adjective may seem strange but I have watched his face, as photographer and friend, too long to miss the clouds that occasionally fleck the familiar sunshine. ~ The award to Mr. Pearson of the Nobel Peace Prize in 1957 was a source of pride to all Canadians regardless of party. I was present in the House of Commons as he received the congratulations of his supporters and opponents alike. His appearance that day stuck in my memory and I resolved to capture it, in a permanent portrait in the Commons chamber which was reproduced in earlier volumes of my portraits. ~ Afterwards I submitted a series of questions to Mr. Pearson in the hope of probing, as it were, his philosophy of international life. I was particularly interested by his interpretation of Canada's position amid the constantly changing problems of the world. 'Canada can always take a disinterested stand, in the sense that she can do what is right irrespective of what anybody else does. This is easier for us because we have no national interests that are continually under examination or challenge at the United Nations. So we do not need to feel superior or smugly virtuous. We have also to remember that in cases of doubt as to what is right or wrong—and most international issues involve doubt in this sense—we have always to take into consideration the importance of co-operating with our friends. We should never break with them unless we are absolutely sure we are right. On the other hand if we follow the United Kingdom or the United States automatically, any influence we have with them or in the international community would soon disappear.' ~ This likeness is of a Pearson eight years older and Prime Minister of his country—a man who even in that position succeeded in rising above the excesses of partisanship. Perhaps he will be best remembered for his achievements in this role, which included the next-to-impossible accomplishment of securing for Canada her own distinctive flag. Yet even in his office as national leader, a room dominated by the fine wooden carving of the country's arms, a globe close at hand is a reminder of continuing pervasive interest in the welfare of the entire world.

Pablo Picasso

Pseudonym of Pablo Ruiz; Spanish painter. Born (1881) and educated in Barcelona; a resident of France most of his adult life. Began to work in Paris in 1901; founded and led the Cubist School; designer for Diaghilev Ballet 1917–27; Director of Prado Gallery, Madrid, 1936–9. Lenin Peace Prize, 1962. Among his paintings are: 'Les Arlequins,' 'L'Aveugle,' 'La Famille du singe,' 'Massacre in Korea,' 'War and Peace,' and portraits of Stravinsky, Cocteau, Apollinaire, and Max Jacob. Also noted for his graphics. Now lives near Cannes.

'Picasso,' his friends had told me, 'doesn't care.' This, as I found to my sorrow, is quite true. A remarkable artist, who has kept the world of art on tip-toes and in a state of nervous exhaustion for years, he has the rare quality of simply not caring. Especially about appointments. My own experience was different. When I reached his home in time for our arranged appointment in 1954 I found him out, but he had been delayed by the arrival of relatives at the airport. When he arrived, we made a new appointment, at a local gallery where his ceramics were on display. At the gallery I found everybody sceptical about my appointment: they assured me that it would be futile to set up my equipment since Picasso so seldom kept his engagements. However, I stood firm and, to everyone's amazement, the man whose every act is sensational caused yet another sensation by arriving exactly on time. Moreover, he had dressed up for the occasion. His magnificent new shirt made the attendants shake their heads in wonderment; whatever had come over the old lion? ~ A final surprise was in store. Picasso declared that he had seen my work and it interested him greatly. I would have taken this for mere flattery, in atonement for the previous day's delay, if he had not cited many of my portraits which evidently he had remembered. The sitting went smoothly, yet I am sure that such normality on his part was highly abnormal. ~ During a talk about his work, Picasso argued that the true norm of art must vary with every artist. Each had his own laws. For this reason he objected strenuously to the legend of his artistic anarchy. His work was constructive, not destructive. He was a builder, not a destroyer. If people thought differently, that was because they didn't understand what he was trying to do. He was in fact trying to express his vision of reality and if it differed from other men's visions that was because any reality was real only to one man. It differed, for better or worse, in every human mind. Art, he said, began with the individual. Without him, there could be no art. With countless individuals there would be countless versions of art, of reality.

Jean-Paul Riopelle
C.C.

Canadian painter. Born in Montreal in 1923, but has lived in Paris since 1947. One-man shows in Paris, New York, and London; chosen for the Younger European Painters Exhibition at the Guggenheim Museum, New York, 1953–4. In 1961 his paintings were selected for showing at the 42nd Pittsburgh International Exhibition (inaugurated by Andrew Carnegie to show 'old masters of tomorrow'); his works are in the Tate Gallery of London, the National Gallery of Canada, and in many private collections. He received a Canada Council Medal in 1966 and was created a Companion of the Order of Canada in 1969.

After climbing the stairs to his top-floor rooms in the rue Frémicourt, a working-class district in Paris, I found this Canadian-born painter to be a very natural, robust fellow. There is a courtly and gallant quality about him—a born gentleman in the guise of a rough-hewn cavalier. He welcomed us warmly and immediately opened a bottle of wine, prelude to much good talk. ~ I admired a circular painting hanging over the fireplace; it looked, I remarked, like a rosette in a stained glass window. Riopelle had previously been amusingly critical of the established art critics and he replied to me in the same vein. Jokingly, he said, 'I'll tell you why I did that. Because my dealers insist on evaluating the price of a canvas by the number of square inches in it; for the fun of it, I decided to confuse them and paint one that is round.' ~ Riopelle had been experimenting with new media, and a piece of sculpture he had completed stood beside him as we chatted, which I incorporated into this portrait. This print of this dynamic artist in his environment has since been acquired by the National Gallery of Canada as the first photograph of their newly-formed photographic archives. And Riopelle has painted another round canvas, especially for the Karsh home near Ottawa. ~ Riopelle must be the fastest driver among the world's artists. To sit alongside him as his Bugatti careens along the narrow gravel-strewn French roads is a frighteningly exhilarating experience. ~ He enjoys his life in France, yachting in the Mediterranean, drinking in Montmartre, and helping younger artists by lending them the use of his studio and materials. ~ He is considered by the art critics as a 'French' painter, yet he still draws much sustenance from his French-Canadian background, and remains drawn to Canada, which he visits frequently. ~ Riopelle's method of working is characteristic of the complete man. It is almost as if his art explodes from him. He will go for weeks and even months without painting. Then will come a period of intense, almost frantic activity. He will paint for weeks; he will not eat; he will not sleep; he will cover canvas after canvas with his highly individual, textured interlacings of bright impasto. ~ Only when the compulsive urge is over will his labours also subside—like a comet that has built up energy until it explodes across the sky.

Albert Schweitzer

French missionary-surgeon, founder of Hospital at Lambaréné, Gabon (1913). Born 1875 in Upper Alsace; educated at Universities of Strasbourg, Paris, and Berlin; obtained degrees in philosophy, theology, and medicine. Organist, J. S. Bach Society, Paris, 1903–11, and an expert on Bach's music. Awarded Nobel Peace Prize in 1952. Wrote many books, on his work in Africa, on Bach, on religious subjects, and appeals for peace. Held many honorary degrees. Retired in 1965 as Director of the Hospital at Lambaréné and died there the same year.

It had taken me a long time to meet 'le Grand Docteur.' For several years I had wondered how I should ever reach his home and hospital in Lambaréné, French Equatorial Africa (now Gabon); then by good luck, I found myself in France in 1954 when he was visiting his home town, Gunsbach, in Alsace. ~ When one has read all Dr. Schweitzer's works and long admired him from the distance, one fears that the actual man may fall below the imagined image. But he was all one imagined he would be. I felt at once, as all men do, the presence of a conscious and immense wisdom, the stronger for its utter simplicity. ~ Of course, he said, my wife and I and my assistant must have lunch with him, and it was a luncheon frugal in the extreme. But after luncheon we were served with excellent coffee and I began then to get a glimpse of a universal mind which still had time for the smallest human detail. This coffee, he explained, was made from beans five years old. 'Coffee made from young beans is toxic. After the beans are about five years old they are medicinal, in fact beneficial.' ~ What struck me from the beginning was this man's power to concentrate his mind totally on the business at hand. While the equipment was being prepared he went back to his writing as if he were alone in the room and then, when I was ready, he gave me his full attention. ~ Of course a thousand questions were on my tongue and it was tantalizing to realize that I would not have time to ask a fraction of them. While we talked I watched Dr. Schweitzer closely, especially his hands. They were the fine hands of a musician and a healer. I wished to photograph him holding some books, preferably an album of Bach, but he protested that to use Bach's music for this purpose would be like 'choucroute garnie.' Accordingly, with a shy smile, he brought out some of his own books. And then he revealed a very human side, by declining to be photographed while wearing his spectacles. 'They make me look too old,' he said. ~ It was, of course, my hope not so much to make the portrait that Schweitzer might desire, but to catch him, if possible, at an unconscious moment when perhaps my camera might seize something of those qualities which have made him great as a doctor, musician, philosopher, humanitarian, theologian, and writer. The picture printed here was taken in a moment of meditation. ~ Remembering his tolerance, and his ministrations to the African natives, I asked him how he thought Christ would be received if He were to appear in our time. Dr. Schweitzer looked up at me and in his quiet voice replied, 'People would not understand Him at all.' Which, then, did he consider the most important of the Ten Commandments? He thought about that for a long moment, the granite face was illuminated, the man behind the legend suddenly visible. 'Christ,' he said, 'gave only one Commandment. And that was Love.'

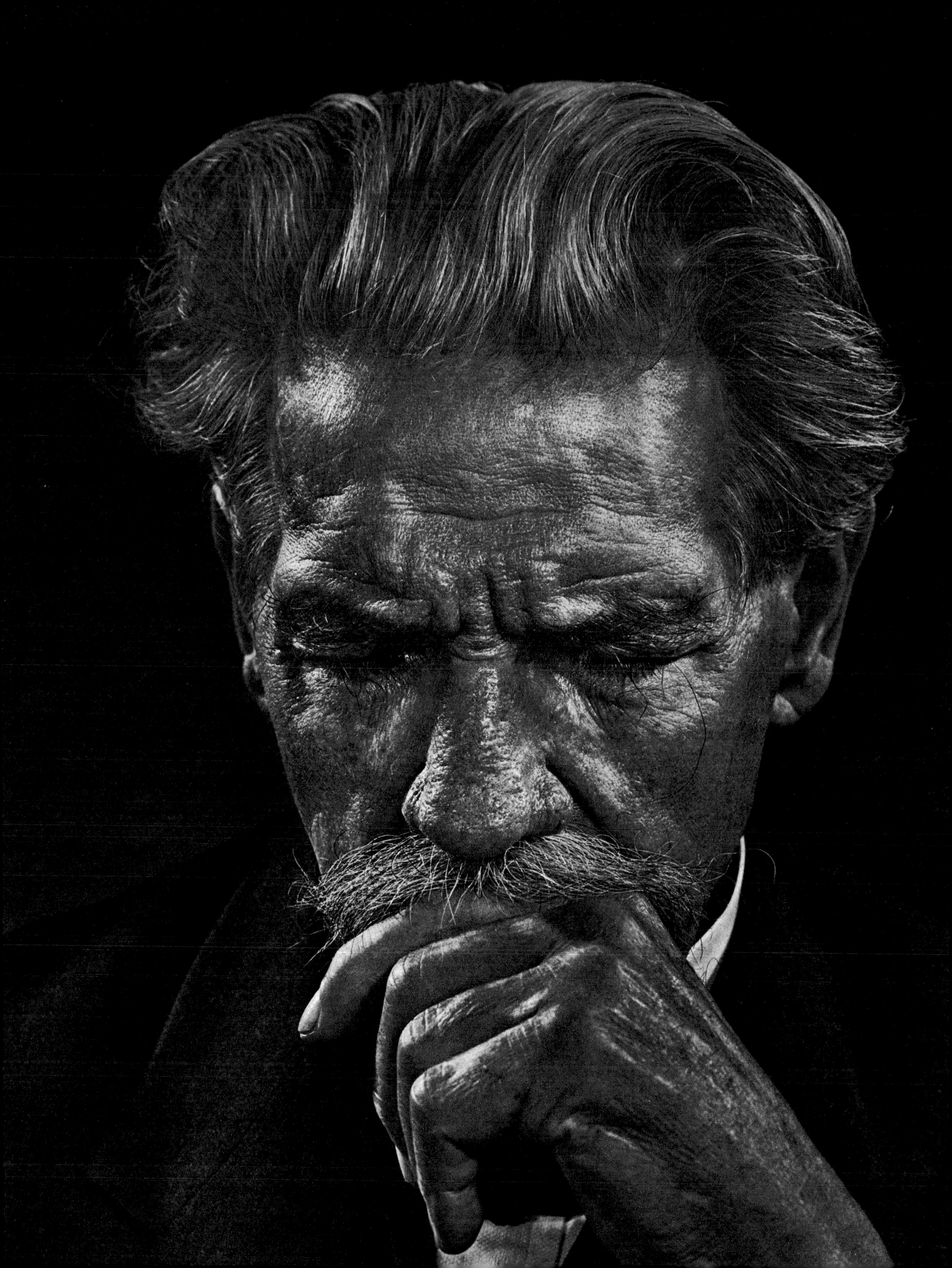

Ravi Shankar

Indian sitar player, teacher, and composer; the first Indian instrumentalist to gain an international reputation and to introduce Indian music to the Western world. Born in Benares, 1920. Among his many compositions have been scores for a number of films, including *Pather Panchali*, *The Flute and the Arrow*, and *Charly*. Encounters in Paris with musicians who had no appreciation of Indian music led to his desire to introduce it to the West, and in 1956 he gave his first recitals in the United States and the United Kingdom. Since then, his recitals and recordings have enjoyed increasing popularity in the West. He has taught at universities in the United States, and in 1967 he opened a branch of his music school in Los Angeles.

There was no difficulty in finding the apartment occupied by Ravi Shankar in the New York hotel where he had invited me to meet him before our photographic session. The fragrance of curry wafting through the corridor was guide enough. ~ I had spent the previous evening at a concert given by this Indian musician at Lincoln Center. He played, on his ancient native stringed instrument called the sitar, the music of Indian *ragas*, built on exotic notes, fresh with constant improvisation on the basic melodies. The artist's verbal introductions added much to one's enjoyment and understanding. No less fascinating was the rapport he quickly established with his audience, who clustered round him after the concert. They were very different from the traditionally dressed concert-going audiences I was accustomed to find at that hall: here was the youth of today, obviously disciples of Shankar. His music has intrigued many Western devotees in recent years, the best-known among them including such musical extremes as the Beatles and the classical violinist, Yehudi Menuhin, with whom he has cut records. ~ Ravi Shankar performs in public on a broad platform covered with Indian throws. In my New York apartment, where we went for his portrait, I opened a table and covered it with one of these throws. He immediately removed his shoes; barefooted, he climbed up and sat cross-legged, with his sitar. Next he took off his wrist watch, as if to remove all traces of contemporary Western civilization, and laid it beside him. He took a little container of oil and moistened the tips of his fingers with oil-soaked cotton, as he tuned the strings. And then he began to play. He performed as if my studio were a temple. ~ He played for the rest of the sitting almost without interruption. We were far from New York; we were in India, enchanted by themes of summer, of darkness, of war, of love. All the time his remarkable, expressive face echoed the sentiment of the music. It was a perfect empathy of man and instrument.

George Bernard Shaw

Irish playwright, novelist, critic, and philosopher; one of the founders of the Fabian Society, 1884. Born in Dublin, 1856; died at Ayot St. Lawrence, England, 1950. Educated at Wesley College, Dublin, and received some training in music and painting at home. Went to London, 1876. Began to come into prominence in 1885 as music critic (writing under the pseudonym Corno di Bassetto for the *Star* and later the *World*), drama critic, book-reviewer, and propagandist for socialism. Awarded the Nobel Prize for Literature, 1925. His published works include some fifty plays and many novels, essays, treatises, etc. Best known among these are perhaps the plays *St. Joan, Major Barbara, Pygmalion, Arms and the Man, The Doctor's Dilemma,* and *Heartbreak House,* and the essays *The Perfect Wagnerite* and *The Intelligent Woman's Guide to Socialism.*

Though this portrait appeared in my earlier book, I include it here for two reasons: no collection which includes modern thinkers would be complete without G.B.S.; and I happen to like my photograph of him. Happily Shaw shared that opinion. ~ I'm glad he liked it but I must say every obstacle was in my way when I first met him in 1943. To begin with, his secretary laid down drastic and quite impossible terms. I was to have five minutes only with the great man. There were to be no lights. I could use nothing but a 'miniature camera.' While I was arguing vainly Shaw himself came bursting into the room with the energy of a young man, though he was then almost ninety years old. His manner, his penetrating old eyes, his bristling beard, and crisp speech were all designed to awe me and, in the beginning, they succeeded. Shaw said he could see no reason why I should photograph him anyway. I explained that the Government of Canada wished to have a good portrait of him in the National Archives at Ottawa. 'Since when,' he retorted, 'does the Canadian Government know a good picture when it sees one? And in any case why did they not commission Augustus John at a thousand guineas and make sure of the job? If John did it, the job would be good—or at any rate everybody would think so.' Plucking up my courage, I suggested that perhaps I had been assigned to make the portrait for that same reason. ~ In the end I had all the time I wanted and I think Shaw enjoyed himself. For he was a better actor than many who appeared in his plays and he obviously loved to act. His favourite role seemed to be that of a sort of harmless Mephistopheles, or the grumpy wicked uncle with a heart of gold. After he had tested me with preliminary terror we got along beautifully. ~ He said I might make a good picture of him, but none as good as the picture he had seen at a recent dinner party. There he had glimpsed, over the shoulder of his hostess, what he took to be a perfect portrait of himself—cruel, you understand, a diabolical caricature but absolutely true. He had pushed by the lady, approached that living image, and found that he was looking into a mirror! The old man peered at me quizzically to see if I appreciated his little joke. It was then that I caught him in my portrait. ~ Later on, a noted British journalist asked me to prepare a copy of this picture which he proposed to have autographed by Shaw. To his chagrin, he received the picture with Shaw's signature scrawled on the back of it. When asked for an explanation Shaw replied: 'I was careful to make sure that my signature should not distract from my face.' Nothing could, I think, distract from that face.

Jean Julius Sibelius

Finnish composer (1865–1957). Educated at Helsinki University and at Berlin and Vienna Conservatories. In 1897 Finland gave him a life grant on which he was able to retire and devote himself to creative work. His music is profoundly individual, national, and poetic in character. His works, among the best known of which are *Finlandia* and *The Swan of Tuonela,* include seven symphonies, a violin concerto, about two hundred compositions for piano and over a hundred songs. Held many honorary degrees.

One day when I was photographing an official of Shell Oil, London, the telephone rang. 'Helsinki on the line,' a secretary said. The official apologized for the interruption. 'On the contrary,' I said, 'Helsinki has a magic sound in my ear.' I told him of my long but thwarted ambition to photograph Sibelius. Wires were soon humming, both telephonic and telegraphic, between the British and Finnish capitals and soon afterwards I found myself on the threshold of a simple house in Jarvenpaa, near Helsinki, a house built for Sibelius by a grateful nation, a shrine for all lovers of music. ~ The man who ushered me into his home in 1949 was well into his eighties, and near the end of his life. His hands shook but his mind was wonderfully alert, and he told me that he followed the news of the world in careful detail. ~ We spent a leisurely day of photography punctuated, at intervals, with a break for coffee, cakes, and brandy. Sibelius would call for a toast and then raise an empty glass. 'You see,' he explained, 'I never drink before dinner.' He seemed to be a happy man full of infectious laughter. His little jokes were uttered in French, since I had no Finnish and he little English, but sometimes, stuck for a word, he appealed to one of his daughters, who translated for him. ~ Towards the end of the day when Sibelius appeared fatigued I told him a little story. During the Russo-Finnish war, I said, there were many Finns cutting timber in the Canadian North and, hearing the dire news from home, they brooded and slackened in their work. Production in the camps began to drop. The foreman, with sudden inspiration, acquired a recording of *Finlandia* and piped it to the loggers in the woods. Immediately, the output of timber doubled. Sibelius rocked with mirth. 'You're fantastic!' he cried, 'one never gets tired working with you.' ~ I was not satisfied with that day's work, however, and suggested another sitting. He agreed, and I returned next morning when the portrait printed here was made. ~ Before leaving I presented him with various gifts entrusted to me by some of his admirers in England. As Sibelius said, with another chuckle, these introductory offerings should have been made at the first, not the last moment. He accepted them all with delight. ~ When he said good-bye a barefoot, tow-headed boy of five years appeared from nowhere, the composer's great-grandson, and stood before the old man with his hands clasped as if in worship. The sun poured over the profile of these two, the very young and the very old, destiny yet ahead and destiny fulfilled. Nothing could have done justice to the flaxen hair of the child, to the gentleness of the aged man. Some pictures are better left in memory alone.

Edward Steichen

American photographer. Born in Luxembourg, 1879; family emigrated to the United States when he was three. Studied painting in Paris for two years, and has since spent periods of his life in France. Served in both World Wars, and in 1946 was in command of all U.S. Navy combat photography. He assembled 'The Family of Man' exhibition, consisting of over 500 photographs, which opened in January 1955 and in the next nine years was seen by more than nine million people in 69 countries. Among his numerous awards have been the U.S. Camera Achievement Award (1945, 1949, and 1963), the Premier Award of the Photographic Society of Great Britain (1961), and the U.S. Presidential Medal of Freedom (1964).

'To every branch of photography he has brought his own inventive genius, and pioneered in establishing photography as an art.' So reads my caption under the portrait of the venerable photographer, Edward Steichen, in my one-man photographic exhibition, 'Men Who Make Our World.' ~ When I was a young and struggling photographer, I turned eagerly every month to his pages in the magazine *Vanity Fair* for inspiration. The first time I photographed this giant, during the Second World War, I was very nervous and Steichen, understanding this, was especially encouraging. During the intervening years Steichen's face took on the quality of an Old Testament prophet, and I was anxious to record what endless, restless experimentation, deep thought, and photographic innovation had etched. ~ The patriarch of American photography was nearing his 90th year when this portrait was taken in 1967 at his home in West Reading, Connecticut. He was still erect and vital, and he walked all the way to his greenhouses of prize-winning delphiniums to greet us. ~ Steichen stopped frequently to pet his two beloved dogs, a soulful three-legged beagle appropriately named Tripod, and an enormous bumptious Irish wolfhound, Fintan. We walked together around the property, and Steichen knew and loved every leaf and tree. His botanical knowledge was encyclopaedic. ~ Steichen's home is almost cantilevered over a small lake which reminded me of the series of paintings of water lilies by Claude Monet. Had he ever photographed the French Impressionist? 'How strange you ask,' Steichen replied. 'As a young man in Paris I did once go to Monet's home. I took the long train ride to the country on an extremely hot summer day, lugging many pounds of heavy camera equipment on my back. But when I got to Monet's front door, I couldn't summon up the courage to ring the bell. Three times I reached for the bell rope, and three times I withdrew my hand. I was so intimidated by the thought of that great man, I carried everything home again without a picture.' It is remarkable to think that so daring a photographer could ever have been so timid. ~ During that walk he took his first photograph in many years, of my wife and me against a background of magnolia blossoms. On that occasion, I cheerfully acted as his 'camera assistant.' The late afternoon of our visit was grey and rainy. My wife remarked, 'What a pity it is not a beautiful day.' Steichen looked at her with infinite compassion, touched her arm and, half-smiling, said, '*Every* day of life *is* a beautiful day.' ~ Over dinner, we talked about the future of photography and about the education of young photographers in particular. Steichen said 'Photography is both extremely difficult and extremely easy.' To set a lens opening, to press a button—these are technical operations and can be learned. But to capture a mood or inner spirit demands a creative insight and a searching eye. I, too, have always hoped that young photographers would cultivate an interest in the humanities and become well-rounded human beings. ~ Two weeks later, there arrived in the mail a gift from Steichen—three of his most famous original prints: the definitive portrait of Greta Garbo with her hair pulled back, the montage of Rodin contemplating his famous sculpture, 'The Thinker,' and the revealing portrait of the tycoon, J. P. Morgan. Steichen's inscription I shall always treasure: 'With remembrance of a fine day of work and play—with affection and devotion to my distinguished colleague, Yousuf Karsh.'

John Ernst Steinbeck

American novelist of German and Northern Irish descent; born in California in 1902; died in December 1968. Educated at Stanford University. Much of his work is a reflection of his native district, the Californian interior valleys and the Monterey coast; had a thorough knowledge of marine biology. Tried his hand at many jobs; he made his name in literature with *Grapes of Wrath*, which won the 1939 Pulitzer Prize. Other books include: *Tortilla Flat, Of Mice and Men, Cannery Row, The Moon is Down, East of Eden,* and *The Short Reign of Pippin IV*. In 1943, he went to Europe as correspondent for the *New York Herald Tribune*. After World War II, he travelled extensively, writing articles and reports for various magazines and newspapers. Nobel Prize for Literature, 1962.

The American author who writes of exceedingly earthy characters maintained in Paris a very elegant address. The gate was opened for me, in 1954, by a butler in black coat and striped trousers. ~ There were, however, difficulties in this impressive setting. Sunshine poured into the room, curtains had to be changed, and the electricity supply, as usual in the eccentric power system of France, proved insufficient. Moreover, a continuous stream of people poured through the room—the author's wife, his children one after the other, and his secretary. When the procession was interrupted for a moment I seized the chance, abandoned the French current, and took this portrait with electronic lights. ~ Mr. Steinbeck had talked little during the sitting. His mind was on his own business and on the many urgent questions brought by his secretary. It seemed that a craftsman skilled in revealing the character of other people guarded himself jealously from prying eyes—that here was a courteous but reticent man who did not wear his heart on his sleeve. However, over refreshments served on the terrace, he thawed somewhat and volunteered an amusing little story to prove, as he said, how difficult it sometimes is to be the wife of a celebrity. Mr. and Mrs. Steinbeck, it appeared, had been entertained recently at a large reception of some sort when Zsa Zsa Gabor, the impetuous movie star from Hungary and Hollywood, arrived in her usual flutter. She caught sight of Mr. Steinbeck and rushed at him, oozing charm. 'But John,' she purred, 'you are the one man I have wanted to meet for, oh so long!' Then she launched into what Steinbeck called 'a very intimate conversation,' ignoring everyone else around her. Finally, Mrs. Steinbeck could endure this invasion no longer. She thrust herself between Steinbeck and Gabor and announced, in a cold voice: 'Miss Gabor, I am Mrs. Steinbeck.' That, apparently, ended that. At the recollection, Steinbeck permitted himself a rumble of laughter. I saw in him then for the first time, a long way from his home, some of the qualities of the life in his books.

Igor Stravinsky

Russian-born composer who has been an American citizen since 1945. Born St. Petersburg 1882; studied law at St. Petersburg University and music under Rimski-Korsakov. Naturalized French subject in 1934. Compositions include: *L'Oiseau de feu, Petrouchka, Le Sacre du printemps, Orpheus,* several symphonies and concertos, and ballet music. In 1962, after an absence of 48 years, he returned to his native land to conduct his own works at the invitation of the government of the U.S.S.R., and received a hero's welcome.

It has been said by his good friend Aldous Huxley that Igor Stravinsky is one of those happy intellectual amphibians who seem to be at home on the dry land of words or in the ocean of music. So I found him. But his words were not dry, if that word means dull. On the contrary, speaking in a free mixture of English and French, he entertained my wife and myself in California, in 1956, with a one-man symphony of conversation, witty and wise. ~ Before getting down to work, he said, we must have refreshment and relaxation. Whether working or relaxed, Stravinsky does not exhibit any of the so-called artistic temperament. However, he did restrict the rooms which could be used for photography. Indeed, the space at my disposal was so small that I said I hoped in the next world I would enjoy a little more elbow room. To which he replied: 'Not only you, Mr. Karsh!' ~ Like some of the other composers I have photographed, Stravinsky complained that orchestra conductors in general never asked composers how their work should be played. They believed they knew better than the men who wrote it the proper method of rendition. Yet most conductors didn't understand eighteenth-century music at all. They thought even Bach should be played in a romantic style which was never his intention. ~ Then Stravinsky took off, with acidulous eloquence, about music critics. Few of them, he said, were really qualified musicians, but they had successfully created a cult of the conductor, regardless of merit. As a result, many conductors had become little more than showmen. 'It's easier, you know,' he remarked, 'to become a critic of writing or painting than of music. Everyone can read or look at a painting but few of the music critics can read music properly.' ~ He talked at length about music recordings which, he admitted, had improved greatly in a mechanical sense. But that did not necessarily mean improved music. Some of the older records were by far the best musically. ~ Stravinsky is one of the few creative artists of my acquaintance who shows a deep interest in his wife's work. Madame Stravinsky, a painter of talent, was unfortunately absent at the moment but Stravinsky observed, with obvious pride, that she was attending an exhibition of her work at Santa Barbara. ~ He has a strong admiration also for the artists of the written word. In his little library he showed me some photographs of Tolstoi, Verlaine, T. S. Eliot, Aldous and Julian Huxley, and Virginia Woolf, among others. ~ I also discovered that he admires and is a connoisseur of tobacco. Wherever he goes, he told me, he carries his own cigarettes, made by an Armenian in the United States, of Turkish tobacco and English paper. ~ In everything, I thought, this man is a perfectionist, especially in his work. When I expressed my own pleasure in it he quoted from Oscar Wilde in French: 'Un homme n'est vraiment intelligent que par son travail.'

The Rt. Hon. Pierre Elliott Trudeau
P.C.

Prime Minister of Canada since April 1968. Born in Montreal, 1919. Studied at University of Montreal, Harvard University, University of Paris, London School of Economics. As a lawyer, specialized in labour law and civil liberties cases. Co-founder of *Cité Libre*, a monthly review. In 1961, appointed Associate Professor of Law, University of Montreal. Elected to the House of Commons from Mont Royal, 1965; Parliamentary Secretary to the Prime Minister, 1966–7; Attorney-General and Minister of Justice, April 1967 until his election as Leader of the Liberal Party, April 1968. The Liberal Party under his leadership was returned to power in the general election of June 1968.

The public personality of Canada's Prime Minister took the country by storm and occasioned waves of 'Trudeaumania' which—after three years in office and many crises later—have not completely subsided. Mr. Trudeau is among the most frank of all politicians I have ever photographed. He speaks his mind with responsibility, but without unnecessary caution. He is blessed with a good sense of humour, and has a remarkable memory for persons and events. And when he does speak directly to you, one feels immediately the force and charm which have been described as charisma. ~ But more than just a personality, Mr. Trudeau is a modern philosopher-king, logical, pragmatic, trying to keep his country together and build in it what he calls the 'Just Society.' ~ I caught a glimpse of the strains his aspirations impose on a day when the Catholicos of the Armenian Church, Koran, visited Ottawa with the church's highest honour to confer on the Prime Minister. There was a political crisis, and it was six o'clock before Mr. Trudeau could see him. I was present. The Prime Minister appeared absolutely exhausted. When he had received the beautiful medal, he remarked with a tired smile, 'It was particularly welcome on this hard day to have some spiritual association. It helps make one forget the trials and tribulations.' At an investiture ceremony for the Order of Canada, Canada's highest award, at Government House, where the Governor General and all the recipients were in the most formal dress, he arrived late in business suit. 'Well,' he said immediately, 'I must be the only hero who is not appropriately dressed.' ~ This photograph was taken a few months after he took over the government leadership, at his official Ottawa residence, 24 Sussex Street. We sat and talked first over dessert and coffee. He was very relaxed, very natural. ~ The next evening I returned with the proofs. He was pleased with this portrait in particular. 'If they will only let me use it as my official photograph,' he said. I asked him who else should choose? Was he not the Prime Minister? (And, though I did not add this, one who is generally understood to have his way?) Yet, when the ultimate decision was made, officialdom selected another of the portraits. ~ This one seems to capture both sides of the man. The leather coat, the symbol of the swinger—his popular image—is almost belied by the very introspective, extremely cerebral quality of the features. They suggest more than cool detachment, they suggest a reluctance, almost a fear of human involvement. Underneath all, Pierre Elliott Trudeau must be one of the most private men who has ever played so great a part in Canadian public life.

Tennessee Williams

American playwright. Born 1914; educated at Universities of Missouri, Iowa, and Washington (St. Louis). Awarded a Rockefeller Fellowship in 1940 for playwriting; in 1943 received a $1,000 grant from the National Institute of Arts and Letters and won Pulitzer Prizes in 1948 and 1955. His plays include: *The Glass Menagerie, A Streetcar Named Desire, Summer and Smoke, The Rose Tattoo, Cat on a Hot Tin Roof, Camino Real, The Night of the Iguana;* he has also written many successful film plays.

Tennessee Williams' reply to my desire to photograph him was enthusiastic and spontaneous, like his plays. We met in his small New York apartment in 1956 and decided that the portrait should be made in his own environment, and I came to realize that this jovial, homespun man contained a tumultuous talent and a soul seldom at peace. ~ Superficially, the plot for this sitting—a sort of minor play rather on the comic side, with Mr. Williams as the comedian and the photographer as his foil—was quite perfect. I had found the master in the scene of his work, surrounded by his typewriter, his manuscript, and his ever present glass of Scotch. Moreover, he seemed to be surrounded by invisible friends. His telephone was constantly ringing as if for the deliberate purpose of distracting me. ~ His obvious desire to co-operate with me and the feigned calm I can sometimes command in a pinch enabled us, however, to deal with invisible friends—and some visible ones—and to get on with the portrait. ~ I asked him whom he considered the greatest American actress. He mentioned no woman born in America but remarked that Anna Magnani, the Italian, had acted in American movies and therefore might be technically within my definition. And he left no doubt that he considered her the greatest living member of her profession. It was for her, he said, that he had specially written *The Rose Tattoo.* ~ At the moment he was working on *Orpheus Descending*, which had been a failure on its first presentation. 'It was performed,' he told me, 'only once, before a Boston audience, and the critics decided it should expire —and it did.' He was therefore rewriting it. ~ At last the portrait was done and when I showed it to some of my friends they remarked that it looked exactly like Williams' plays. Perhaps. At any rate, the playwright's deceptive ease of manner, his informal speech, and carefree air reminded me of various characters made by his pen—ordinary-looking men hiding an unsuspected fury which invariably erupts on the stage, often in tragedy. ~ As Mr. Williams admitted rather shyly to me, and as he has written in moments of candour, he is a man burning with a sense of life and desperate to communicate it somehow to his fellows. He cannot communicate it freely in conversation because, he says, there is a certain sense of social restraint even among friends meeting face to face; to the great, dark, faceless audience of the theatre he can at last speak freely without any reticence. ~ The public knows with what power and sometimes with what nobility he can thus speak. I hope this portrait catches at least a spark of that volcanic inward fire which makes each of his plays a sort of spiritual convulsion and leaves the audience limp with spent emotion.